ESU Framework

Performance Scales for English Language Examinations

Brendan J. Carroll
and Richard West

Longman

ENGLISH-SPEAKING UNION

Longman Group UK Limited,
Longman House, Burnt Mill, Harlow,
Essex CM20 2JE, England
and Associated Companies throughout the world.

First published 1989

Set in 10/11pt Aldus Times

Printed in Great Britain
by The Eastern Press Limited, London and Reading

ISBN 0 582 03161 3

Contents

Preface

Although founded in 1918 to promote goodwill and understanding amongst English speaking peoples, it was not until the 1970s that the English-Speaking Union began to take a specific interest in the language as such. An English Language Committee* was formed with many of the most distinguished professors and teachers of English, with HRH The Duke of Edinburgh as Chairman. Shortly afterwards two annual competitions were started to stimulate new ideas in the learning and teaching of English, one for unpublished manuscripts and the other for published works. A number of conferences, lectures and research projects were organised with particular reference to creating new kinds of basic English for use in spheres like the sea, the air and science.

About the same time a group of representatives from the British Council, the English-Speaking Union and the Association of Recognised English Language Schools was invited to take part in a 'yardstick' conference in Princeton, USA, organised by the Educational Testing Service. The concept of a 'yardstick' for measuring standards of English was discussed at great length but no concrete developments emerged.

In 1984 I approached Reed International for sponsorship for a 'yardstick' project and as a result was able to bring together a small team to work under the banner of the English-Speaking Union. At that stage the cognoscenti were very sceptical about the possibility of creating a framework, not only because of its inherent difficulties, but because of the problem of getting all the appropriate bodies to cooperate.

Nevertheless, the research went ahead and seven of the major examining bodies did cooperate and the first report was produced. It was so well received by the EFL profession that we decided to go ahead and try to cover all the major examining bodies. This book is proof that we did succeed in getting all the bodies to work together under the aegis of the English-Speaking Union and I am indebted to Brendan Carroll and Richard West whose sensitivity in working with individual bodies made the whole project possible. We are, of course, conscious that new tests and examinations are being devised all the time and we hope to bring it up-to-date every two years or so. Meantime the book is supplemented by a chart, which will help newcomers to find their way around the maze of examining bodies and tests.

This book was designed to help students of English around the world by simplifying and rationalising the testing system. It will also have effects on the academic and business institutions which hope to take them in. It could well make ripples in areas we have not yet envisaged.

In pursuing this project over the last four years or so I have been conscious of the constant support of the English-Speaking Union's English Language committee, the British Council and the BBC. I would also like to thank:

The fifteen Examining Boards for their support, both in helping to finance the project and in being ready sources of information about their examinations. The Special Interest Group in Testing of the International Association of Teachers of English as a Foreign Language (IATEFL) and, in particular, Gill Westaway, the group co-ordinator. Christopher Yates, Director of ELTDU for his participation in the initial phase and valuable advice thereafter. The Controller and staff of the British Council's English Language and Literature Division, especially Dr Peter Hargreaves. The staff of the

Education Department of the English-Speaking Union for administrative back-up.
Patricia Carroll for her sustained assistance in data analysis and typing both the initial report and the present book.

H. D. Hicks

Deputy Director-General/Director of Education

English-Speaking Union

HRH The Duke of Edinburgh, Chairman of the English Language Committee, Lord Pym, Chairman of the English-Speaking Union of the Commonwealth, and Mr David Hicks, Deputy Director-General of the English-Speaking Union looking at an early draft of the Framework Chart in Buckingham Palace.

BUCKINGHAM PALACE.

As modern communication techniques make the world smaller, the need for a common language becomes more urgent. In previous ages Latin and French provided this facility and attempts to create an artificial language have not had much success. Today, for a host of reasons, more than a thousand million people have come to use English as their first or second language and many more young people are seeing the advantage of learning it.

The problem faced by all learners of English as a second language is the large number of examining bodies, each offering a bewildering variety of tests and certificates. Not unnaturally, this causes considerable confusion about the significance of such qualifications, with the result that much time and money can be wasted by both students and teaching institutions.

To help solve this problem, the English-Speaking Union brought together the major examining bodies and between them they have produced this book. I very much hope that it will help to simplify and to rationalise the learning and testing of English around the world and introduce a comprehensive standard of assessment of language competence.

Philip

1989

Chapter 1
Introduction to Framework

Why do we need an examination framework?

At present, an overseas student wishing to take an examination in English as a Foreign Language is faced with a truly bewildering range of options. The many Examining Boards covering this field each produce several separate tests, many of which are further subdivided into grades. The number of possible options runs into hundreds. Further confusion is caused by the variety of names given to these grades - First, Second or Third may be the choice of one Board; Pass, Credit or Distinction that of another; and others may choose Preliminary, Intermediate or Higher grades for their Certificates. How can students decide which is the most appropriate examination for them to take? And how does a future employer find out from all this confusing information just what standard of English has been acquired by an applicant presenting a Certificate? All this rich diversity means, of course, that a student's needs are well catered for. The sheer complexity, however, can easily confuse learners, teachers and employers when they wish to judge the significance or value of any of the examinations. In Britain, examination bodies, with their tradition of autonomy, have tended to work independently of each other and have thus produced a host of examinations with all the advantages and disadvantages which that implies.

Imagine the dilemma facing a young person from Tokyo, say, who has the chance of working for a bank in London as long as his or her standard of English is acceptable. There are at least ten Boards which can examine this kind of language proficiency. How can this young person decide which Certificate and which Level is most suitable? And how can the Bank know what the possession of any Certificate means in terms of his/her command of language to work in their London branch? These are the types of question we have been studying for some time and which we hope to answer in this book for the benefit of all kinds of user - teachers, language school organisers, personnel officers in business, admissions officers in colleges and, above all, students of language, working, if necessary, with their teachers.

How the project began

The English-Speaking Union, in its work of promoting the use and understanding of the English language, has been well aware of this perennial problem and, in 1985, set up the 'Framework' project to look at possible ways of creating a frame of description comprehensive enough to describe and compare the examinations of seven of the main English Language boards. If it were possible to devise such a framework, guidance could then be given to all users of examinations about how to choose the most suitable test for them and how to interpret its results. In 1986, the first stage of this project was completed and an optimistic feasibility report was submitted. Encouraged by the results of this initial study, the English-Speaking Union decided to go ahead with a further stage of the project, the number of co-operating bodies being increased from the initial seven to fifteen of the principal British examination boards in English as an International Language.

After two years of intensive work, the full Framework description, with guidelines about how to use it, has now been prepared. A descriptive frame has been produced which harmonises the various elements of the present examination system, preserving its diversity but greatly reducing the possibilities for confusion. This harmonisation has been done by devising a model which describes each examination in a standard way, drawing on a series of performance scales or 'Yardsticks'. A Nine-point Scale has been produced against which users will be able to relate the level of each examination and, at the same time, compare the content and coverage of all the examinations we have described.

The publications

The Framework project will give you guidance about the examinations of the seventeen co-operating boards by means of several publications, each one describing the examinations at a different level of detail:

- ***The ESU Framework*** (Longman 1989): the present book, which gives a full account of the Framework and its applications for teachers, employers, learners, candidates and other examination users.
- ***English Language Examinations from Britain***: a Chart with notes and explanations, showing the main British examinations in a convenient form. The Chart has been produced by the Framework project and will be updated from time to time as required. Enquiries about the Chart may be made to the English-Speaking Union, see the address on p105.
- The ***Longman Guide to English Language Examinations*** (Longman 1989): an updated version of the earlier Pitman Guide giving full descriptions of all current examinations, including those from the USA, France, Germany and Switzerland as well as those from Britain.

In addition, users can refer to the *Syllabuses* and *Handbooks* of the various Examination Boards which give full details of the syllabuses, sample examination questions and the appropriate entry procedures for that particular board.

This present book, *The ESU Framework*, is the key publication of the project and in it we will describe for you:

- The Nine-point Scale; how it is made and how it can be used.
- The Framework model with its five stages for describing language and communication.
- The Chart of Levels, with a description of the various examinations, their coverage in level and content and their availability.
- The Yardsticks; giving descriptions of performance levels for different kinds of activity.
- Descriptions of each of the examinations, with notes about any planned revisions.
- Practical advice on using the Framework materials.
- The implications of Framework in the broader context of language courses, publishing and curriculum development.

There are also a number of Appendices in this book which give further, more detailed information and practical help.

Although, with the completion of this book, we have now achieved the main aim of our project, we hope to continue our collaboration with the boards to give ongoing help to users and to update all publicity materials in the light of experience.

Chapter 2
The Framework Scales

As we have mentioned in Chapter One, there are many and various methods of recording achievement in examinations. Here are some examples from the examinations described in Framework.

The Associated Examining Board has one single examination and gives its results in numbered levels, from 4 down to 1, and the English Language Testing Service similarly awards levels, or bands, but this time from 9 down to 1. The Cambridge Syndicate awards four separate Certificates using a letter system, A B C D E. The Pitman Institute, with five separate examinations, provides a percentage score to accompany their various grades, 60% being a Pass and 75% a First Class Pass, for example. We do not believe that any one of these methods of recording achievement is better or worse than any other, but we can note two points these different systems seem to have in common.

The first is that, in most cases, the systems are internal to an examination, describing language performance in terms of that particular examination and not in terms of actual performance in the outside world.

The second is that the different examination bodies operate quite independently of each other. There is no common ground, even though they are all seeking the same goal - to establish the candidate's level of proficiency in English.

There is little, therefore, to guide an employer, for instance, when interviewing several applicants for a job. The first applicant may have a Grade D certificate from one Board. Others might produce respectively a Level 4, a Very Good Pass, a 75% score or a Distinction from a variety of other Boards. How is the prospective employer to decide which applicant will be the most suitable - on linguistic grounds - for the post? From our experience, we find that an employer usually wants a firm answer to the question, 'What will these applicants be able to do in English if I appoint them to the post?' And our young person from Tokyo will want some assurance about being able to cope with the language demands to be met whilst working and living in London. At present, the sheer diversity of the information available to would-be users of the examinations fails to provide reliable guidance in interpreting results or in providing answers to these questions.

In devising the Framework descriptive system, we have moved towards a solution to these problems in interpreting the results of examinations. By describing each of our examinations in common terms, within a common frame, and using real-world descriptions of language performance, we feel we will be able to help users, whether students, teachers, employers or institutions, to interpret and compare a whole range of examinations. Our young person from Tokyo will, almost at a glance, be able to decide which is the most appropriate examination for that particular purpose, and the Bank in London will be able to decide whether or not a person will 'fill the bill'.

Our essential method for harmonising the examination system has been to make a series of scales, or 'Yardsticks' which we will use to plot a wide range of features of the examinations. The basic pattern is shown in Figure 2.1.

Figure 2.1 The Yardstick Ladder

9	Maximum performance
8	
7	
6	
5	
4	
3	
2	
1	Minimum performance

Each yardstick describes language performance in terms of both quantity and quality. By quantity we mean that a scale has a number of levels, or bands, corresponding to the rungs on a ladder, so that a learner's performance can be described as being, say, at level 4 or 5 on the scale. Accompanying these levels are descriptions of the quality of the language performance which outline briefly and clearly the main features of the performance that can be expected at each level. These 'descriptors' are put in real-world terms that are meant to be intelligible both to teachers and to consumers such as employers and admissions tutors in colleges and universities.

The ESU Framework uses yardsticks with nine levels which range from 'extremely limited command' at Level 1 to a 'fully competent command' at Level 9. The descriptors for these levels reveal steps of increasing linguistic proficiency, as shown in Figure 2.2.

We give examples of full yardsticks later in Chapter 5, but for now please note that all yardsticks are made to the same blueprint and according to the same criteria. In this way, it is possible to create yardsticks which are consistent in their description of language at different degrees of detail, beginning with general or overall proficiency, through one of the skills such as writing, to the specific tasks such as writing business letters. New yardsticks can also be constructed quite easily as new language tasks are introduced, either because they are included in new or revised examinations, or because of the introduction of new communication technologies, such as electronic mail.

The 1 to 9 Scale

It is possible to make Yardsticks using various numbers of levels or bands. We have, in fact, chosen nine levels as we have found that this number is sufficient to cover the entire span of language performance and the complete range of teaching and testing materials needed to teach and examine it. Language learning is frequently thought of as graduating through three phases, often referred to as 'elementary', 'intermediate' and 'advanced'. Performance in each phase can then be broken down and specified as being at, above or below the expected level, so that we have nine levels in all.

Figure 2.2 Extracts from the General Proficiency Yardstick

Level	Descriptors
9	Has a full command of the language, tackling the most difficult tasks with consistent accuracy, fluency, appropriate usage, organisation and comprehension. An exceptional level of mastery, not always reached by native speakers, even quite educated ones.
	Levels 2 to 8
1	Uses a few words or phrases such as common greetings and recognises some public notices or signs. At the lowest level, may only recognise which language is being used.

For the 'advanced' phase, which involves difficult tasks, we look for an acceptable performance at the level laid down by our performance criteria. And similarly with the other two phases, the 'transitional' or 'intermediate', calling on moderately difficult tasks and the elementary, or preliminary, involving relatively simple tasks.

In fact, there are few examinations designed for those at the very lowest ESU level, but there are, of course, many learners at that level, as well as language courses and textbooks to cater for their needs, as we show in Chapter 9, Broader Implications of Framework.

Yardstick applications

Language yardsticks are not new. They were used, for example, in the 1960s by the Foreign Service Institute (FSI) in the United States and the English Language Teaching Development Unit (ELTDU) in Britain. They became widely known after their adoption for the British Council's English Language Testing Service in the 1980s. However, these organisations confine their use of yardsticks to specifying learners' performance in specific tests or examinations. The ESU project attempts a wider application, namely to devise a framework of yardsticks on which many examinations can be plotted - a 'scale of scales'. In this way, we can describe all examinations in common terms using standard yardsticks with real-world descriptors of performance.

The use of standard yardsticks allows us not only to describe examinations in common terms; it also enables us to make indirect comparisons between different examinations. We must always remember that no two examinations are exactly alike in skills coverage, level, technique or area of use and so it is unwise to make a direct comparison between them. This problem - how to compare examinations which may be in many ways unlike - was referred to as the 'chalk and cheese' problem at an early stage in the project. However, if we plot each examination separately on to the ESU yardsticks, it then becomes possible to make indirect comparisons.

Figure 2.3 Yardstick for Indirect Comparison

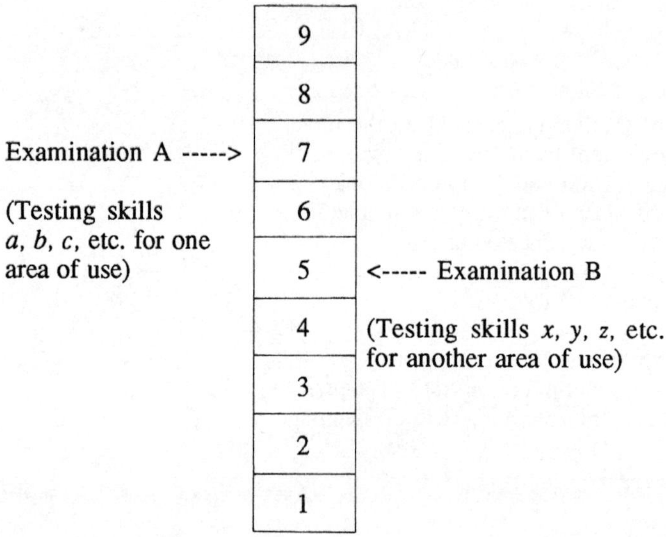

From this example we can see that a learner who has just passed Examination A can be expected to perform at a more sophisticated level than one who has just passed Examination B. In this broad sense, we can say that Examination A demands performances at a higher level than Examination B, whatever the differences in content coverage. Whether or not a candidate who passes Examination A can be expected to pass Examination B can only be decided after a study of these various content factors. In this way we become aware not only of the similarities but also the dissimilarities of the different examinations.

Yardstick construction

When constructing yardsticks to describe differing areas of language performance, we must always work from a common blueprint. The blueprint we adopted will focus on two themes which have been continually referred to by the examining bodies in their various publications. One theme concerns the difficulty of the tasks, which we called 'Inputs'. The other is the adequacy of the candidate's performance, or 'Outputs'. Our basic criteria, then, draw on these two aspects, using three degrees of task difficulty and three degrees of performance adequacy as we show in Figure 2.4. Of course, not all the Boards covered these criteria at every level in the Framework. Indeed, there was a shortage of very difficult, exacting tasks at the top end of the scale and of very easy tasks at the bottom end. Thus, the present examinations tend to cluster at the middle levels from about levels 3 to 7.

We will discuss the rationale for this blueprint and the criteria underlying the descriptors at greater length in Chapter 3.

Figure 2.4 The Yardstick Blueprint

INPUT (task)	OUTPUT (performance)	ESU LEVEL
	above expected level	9
Difficult task	at criterion level	8
	just below expected level	7
	above expected level	6
Moderate task	at criterion level	5
	just below expected level	4
	above expected level	3
Simple task	at criterion level	2
	just below expected level	1

When creating yardsticks to this blueprint, we follow these principles:

- All yardsticks should be produced from the same basic blueprint and all descriptors should use the same criteria. This principle not only ensures consistency from level to level and from one yardstick to another, but also makes the production of new yardsticks relatively simple.
- All yardsticks separate input, the examination task requirement, from output, the learner's performance in fulfilling the task requirement.
- Input tasks are always described at three levels - simple, moderate and difficult.
- Output performance is described in terms of the nine levels, each with its explanatory descriptors.
- Performance is described in positive terms, as far as possible, specifying what learners can be expected to do at a particular level rather than what they cannot do. In this way, even modest performance is valued, as it may well be adequate for a consumer's needs, eg a job in a postal sorting room in a Middle East company may require merely that the employee can read addresses written in English and direct them to the correct company office.
- Performance is described at the level of achievement needed for that particular level, and we assume that performance at that level includes, or subsumes, a mastery of the skills specified for lower levels. So, for example, the performance of a person at level 4 will be described by reference to moderately difficult tasks rather than to the lower-level, simple tasks which have already been specified for the lower stages.

Criteria for Input and Output

We have already referred to the need for the yardstick descriptors to be based on common criteria. Here is a summary of the criteria used both in judging the difficulty of a task, or Input, and the acceptability of a candidate's performance, or Output. In many cases we have made use of the terms used by the Examining Boards. However, the various Boards differed widely in their use of descriptive terms, so we have selected those terms we found useful and have organised them to make a logical framework of criteria as we now show.

Difficulty criteria for Input

Everyone has an idea of what a 'difficult' test is and what an 'easy' test is. In language tests, we find quite a list of features which relate to this difficulty factor. Let us look at a few of these. The most obvious are size, speed and complexity of the set tasks; these features put pressure on candidates to complete the test within the time allowed, assuming that there is a time limit. Tests which call on a wide range of language skills - requiring a command of a wide range of grammar, vocabulary and style items obviously stiffen up their difficulty. A test can also increase its demands if it involves the use of very specialised or unfamiliar topics which need to be treated in great detail and very precisely. And, finally, the conditions of testing can be very rigorous, perhaps with little chance to refer to information sources, such as dictionaries, with little tolerance of mistakes or for opportunities to repair them, with no opportunities for individuality in responses, and possibly accompanied by 'noise' - interference from outside sources or the use of interruptions, unclear instructions - which so often occurs in real-life.

Such are the features of difficulty. An 'easy' test will, of course, be described by features at the other end of the spectrum - it will be short, straightforward, demanding a limited range of skills, using familiar topics in an undemanding way, and with a good deal of tolerance being extended to errors or misunderstandings.

Performance acceptability criteria for Output

When judging the adequacy, or acceptability, of candidates' responses to the tasks they have been set, there are so many possible aspects to look at that we have divided them into three main areas - message, text/interaction and language usage. When judging an essay or an interview, teachers have traditionally looked at these three aspects of performance. They look to find out how well the overall task has been dealt with - whether the necessary message has been conveyed in an essay, or has the interview been properly handled, basically whether the candidate's response has been relevant, clear, coherent, interesting and whether he or she has shown awareness of the reader or listener.

After looking at the overall value of the performance, a rater can then look at the strategies a candidate has used to reach the targets. In an essay, how well the topic has been organised. Is it logical and cohesive? Are the style and layout clear and appropriate to the topic? Does the essay flow? In an interview or group interaction, does the candidate make a suitable contribution to the discussion, speaking fluently in a suitable style and coping well with the ebb and flow of the discussion whilst showing sensitivity to others taking part in it?

Then, one has to look at the way candidates have used language to achieve their goals. Obviously, the accuracy, range and suitability of the language used is important. Various aspects of grammar and vocabulary must be looked at; in essays, spelling and handwriting and in interviews, pronunciation, stress and intonation must be adequate.

In looking at these three rating aspects - message, text/interaction and language usage - there is no clear priority. If the language used is incomprehensible due to inadequate pronunciation, spelling, handwriting or grammar, then there can be no interaction, and no message will be passed. On the other hand, it is of little use to produce correct sentences which do not hang together or deal with the topic being addressed. Ultimately, a judge has to ask , how well has the candidate handled the required task? Obviously, message-handling adequacy is a first essential, but whether the message has been properly handled will depend on the suitability of the language used, at sentence level, and how well these sentences have been put together to achieve the objective required by the task. For a proper rating, then, we believe all three levels of assessment must be considered.

Chapter 3
The Framework Stages

So far, we have been describing in the *Framework Scales*, or Yardsticks, the examination aspects of our project - the various levels and the various task and performance criteria related to them. In this chapter, we will look at those aspects of the language which are being examined, and which we will call the *Framework Stages* of language proficiency.

There are many different types of language examination. Some of them focus on translation, on grammatical and stylistic patterns or on general points of usage. These are often called 'indirect' tests of language proficiency. Other examinations do not explicitly deal with grammar or usage at all but concentrate on real-life tasks, such as using the telephone, writing business letters and taking part in meetings. Such tests are often called 'direct' tests of language proficiency. And, in between these two extremes, is a whole range of examinations which use both direct and indirect types of item.

What we have aimed to do in these circumstances is to devise a model which would describe fairly and accurately this range of examination types. It must be remembered that we were not in the business of inventing afresh a new model of language but were intending to describe accurately and fairly all the examinations within our project, for wholly practical purposes.

The actual model we devised is shown in Figure 3.1. As you can see, the model has five stages, or layers, in increasing order of detail from broad language/communication proficiency down to the many 'enabling' linguistic, functional and test-taking skills.

Here are some explanations of the Five-Stage Framework model.

Stage I: Overall language/communication proficiency

We assume that all language examinations, whatever their nature or specific purpose, are intended to make an evaluation of the candidate's overall proficiency in using language. Different examinations will clearly make this overall evaluation through different means. Some will use direct methods, others indirect methods, or a mixture of both. Nevertheless, if our basic project aim is to be met, there has to be some initial descriptive stage which will accommodate the main features of all the examinations being described. For this reason, the descriptors in our overall Yardstick for Stage I do not separate out the 'four skills' or specify any particular purpose or context of use. It is possible that users will be quite satisfied with this general description of proficiency and will wish to go no further than Framework Stage I using the descriptions given in Chapter 5, Yardstick 1.

Figure 3.1 The Five-Stage Framework Model

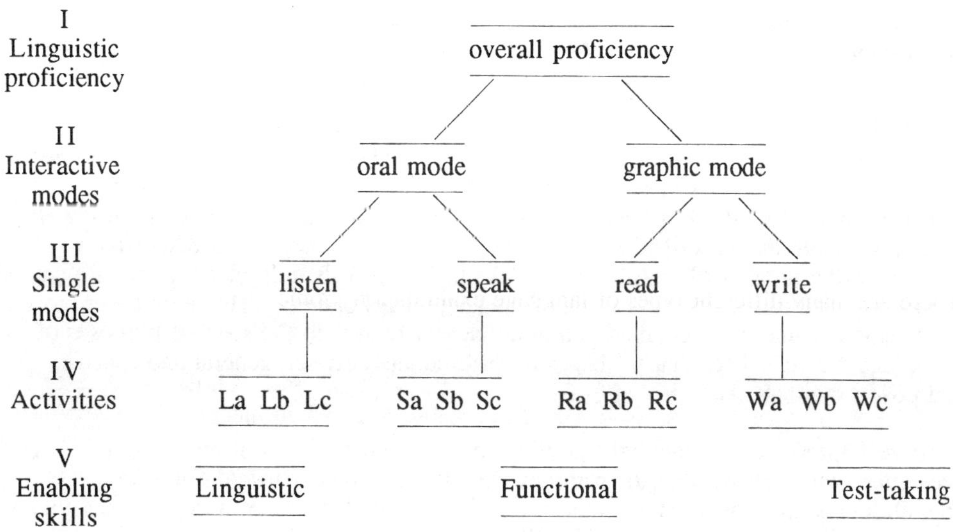

L, S, R, W = listening, speaking, reading, writing

a, b, c = activities mainly in the mode concerned

Stage II: Interactive modes

Our overall proficiency stage now divides into two - the modes of graphic and oral interaction, thus making a broad distinction between written and spoken communication. The level descriptors, therefore, become more specific as can be seen in Yardsticks 2 and 3 in Chapter 5. Many examinations assess both the written and spoken modes but some, such as those of Trinity College and ARELS, concentrate on the spoken mode and others, such as Pitman and Oxford, on the written mode. The relevant yardsticks will show this sort of allocation.

From the user's point of view, it will be useful to have information about this graphic or oral emphasis. For example, some employees, such as airline cabin crew, will require a mainly oral approach. Others, such as library researchers, will rely mainly on the graphic skills. Examinations will then be chosen accordingly.

Stage III: Single modes

At this stage, we diversify into the traditional four skills of reading, writing, listening and speaking. (See Yardsticks 4 to 7 in Chapter 5.) One significant point about this fourfold division is that no examination focusses exclusively on one skill - in fact, it would not be a practical proposition to run an examination on one skill; even an examination for public speaking would need to start with some topic guidance which the candidate would have to read or listen to. In our project, we have studied examinations supposedly in listening which required considerable skills in reading - of instructions and background information, and in writing - to record responses to the items.

In practice, then, we have had to decide which of the skills being tested is the dominant one. It is this dominant skill which dictates which yardstick is to be applied. Teachers and syllabus designers have traditionally viewed language through the four skills, and the Stage III yardsticks will help them by giving them enough detail to match examination content to their teaching situations.

Stage IV: Communication activities

These activities are derived from real-life-operational tasks such as, 'writing business letters', 'taking telephone messages' and 'studying academic texts'. (See Yardsticks 8 to 19 in Chapter 5.) You will have noticed that the number of yardsticks in the first three stages we have just described is finite, numbering one, two and four respectively. However, the number of possible yardsticks in Stage IV is unlimited, so that we can add on as we wish to include new kinds of language tasks or items. The level descriptors at this stage become more detailed and more closely related to the specific purposes of language use. It is here that we begin to differentiate between general and specific-purpose examinations.

The descriptors at this stage will provide valuable information for teachers and course designers who will be able to fit the examinations to their particular course requirements. Employers and admissions officers will also be given more direct guidance for placing applicants in jobs or educational programmes.

Stage V: Enabling skills

At this stage, we include those important skills which underlie a person's performance in real-life; we also consider those particular test-taking skills which, rightly or wrongly, play such an important part in examination success. A command of these 'enabling' skills is indispensable for carrying out any language/communication task although they are not, in themselves, real-life tasks.

We have divided the enabling skills into three main areas: linguistic, such as the grammatical and lexical skills; functional, to handle inter-personal and conceptual activities; and test-taking, or examination, required in responding suitably to the demands of the examination. (See Yardsticks 20 to 22 in Chapter 5.)

Teachers who follow traditional approaches to language learning/teaching will find the descriptors at Stage V, especially those in the linguistic area, of particular relevance.

The descriptive nature of Framework

In devising our model for the Framework Stages, we have constantly kept in mind the requirements of description. The model has not been designed either for evaluation or prescription - it is not a critical one. What we wished to do was to describe accurately and appropriately all the examinations included in the project. In applying the yardstick descriptors, we are not implying an 'order of merit' to the various stages, yardsticks or examinations. We leave it to the user - learner, teacher or employer - to decide which of the language aspects we have described are relevant to their needs and, therefore, which examinations are suitable for them. We consider the Framework to be a descriptive tool to help in this process of selection.

Chapter 4
Using Framework

We have never been under the illusion that devising our Framework was to be a simple task. The problems arising from the diversity of English Language examinations are complex and there are no straightforward solutions to them. We will, however, have made significant progress if we have defined clearly the structure of our two important models - the one, concerning the performance levels and criteria of the Framework Scales, the other, the elements of language description of the Framework Stages. Our next task is to show how these models can be used as practical tools for choosing and interpreting examinations.

A useful starting point in this process is the Chart - *English Language Examinations from Britain*, a large, colourful and comprehensive outline of the examination system we are describing. On the front of the chart we show clearly the Nine-point levels of the various grades of the examinations and a checklist of the features of each examination as well as the addresses and phone numbers of the Boards. On the reverse side of the Chart there is a lot of additional information which will help towards making the right choice of examination and how to follow up with further information about examinations and language courses. You can find the Chart of Levels section of the large chart in Figure 4.1 later in this chapter.

The Chart levels

On the Chart, the first component is the general description of language proficiency, Stage I of the Framework Stage model, in the broadest of terms. The task difficulty aspect is touched on only broadly and mainly in terms of the demands to be met in real-life, from the full pressures and complexities of 'any relevant situation' down to the bare realisation of 'which language is being used'. Of course, Stage I descriptors of such a general kind lack the detail and precision of those of the later stages, but they do provide a useful 'bird's-eye view' of the total scene and they are consistent with the later, more delicate, yardstick descriptors.

The next major component of our Chart is the fitting of the examination grades to the nine ESU levels. Here, we start to be able to appreciate more exactly what all the terms, 'Higher', 'Intermediate', 'Elementary', and Grades 1, 2 and 3, or Levels 6, 7 and 8, etc. might mean. It is interesting to see the range of 'Elementary' grades, one Board awarding this grade at ESU Level 3, another at Level 5. Similarly, 'Intermediate' is to be found respectively in Levels 4, 5 and 6. The numbered grades are very specific to the examination concerned. ESU Level 5, for example, equates to grades 2, 4, 5, 8 and 9 for different certificates. This implies no criticism whatsoever of the Boards awarding the grades, as each Board has a logical and consistent pattern of relating their own grades. But it does reinforce our original diagnosis of the 'truly bewildering' picture of our system of examination grading. At the same time, we can see how the Framework descriptions can help us to bring order to this confusion.

Of course, in interpreting the Chart of Levels, everything rests on the dependability of the chart placements - if they had been merely guesses or even plucked out of the air, they would be poor guidance indeed. Because it is important to establish the credibility of the levels we gave to the various certificates, we carried out a carefully-designed 'verification' procedure. The full results of this exercise are described in Appendix C, but for those not concerned with its details and statistical results, we now give a summary of the main points.

What we wanted to do was to choose, by statistical means, a panel of reliable judges who would rate a set of essays and interviews according to the ESU Nine-point Scales. For example, one essay's average ratings might be, say, 8.5, another's, 5.3, another's 2.6, and so on. These sets of writing and speech samples would then be sent to the Boards who would judge them according to their own criteria. We would then equate the certificate grades with the ESU levels. One Board assessed an essay rated 8.0 on the ESU scale as being a pass at their Diploma level; another essay, rated at 5.5 was given a Pass at Higher Certificate level; and a third rated 3.6 was given a Pass at Elementary Certificate level. We then checked the statistical findings against the subjective estimates which the Boards had agreed with us some time before, and made adjustments to the levels as necessary.

Naturally, even though care was taken to establish high reliability figures - the average correlation indices being in the region of 0.95 for the ESU panel - there is still room for statistical variation, so we are not treating these equivalencies as perfect. It is also true that rating distributions of the kind of material we were judging do tend to give inflated correlation indices, so we must be careful about making absolute judgements of the quoted indices. Nevertheless, we have collected a fair amount of statistical evidence to back up the examination level equivalents we have published in the Chart and which we show in Figure 4.1 on pages 16-19.

We can relate these 9 levels to the various criteria of the Framework input and output model. Our top band of performer, at Level 9, is expected to carry out *difficult* language tasks which range from Levels 7 to 9. At Level 8, he or she will cope effectively. At Level 7, there will be some shortfall in performance, with a few lapses here and there but the proficiency is just about enough to handle the tasks given. As it happens, Level 7 is generally accepted by Universities and businesses as evidence of being likely to cope with study and work in the medium of English.

The performer at the *moderately difficult* task levels of 4, 5 and 6 are given a large coverage by the Boards' examinations. At Level 5, one would expect a useful working knowledge of the language, although there will be major problems in handling 'communication in the raw'. This middle group of bands will represent a fair proficiency in 'getting about' in the language. It is probable that many language learners neither move above this area nor aim to do so.

At the lowest level of difficulty, in the *simple* task levels of 1, 2 and 3, the best one can expect is a command of language sufficient to meet basic needs and even then there will often be communication blocks. Levels 2 and 3 will often be the aim of casual visitors and tourists who will find this level of command a useful asset on their travels. Level 1, however, offers very little in the way of communication.

Examination areas of use

In the Chart, you can see that the Examinations are grouped, from left to right, in three main types: General/Social English, Business English, and Study/Training English. It has not been possible to make a clear distinction between 'General' and 'Social' English. Some examinations have clearly specified their purpose in such terms as 'Social survival in English-using contexts'; others include these contexts but add other topics to give a wider coverage including English Literature or matters of international interest such as Space Travel - not, you will agree, uniquely necessary for Social Survival. If you wish to find out more precisely the aims of any particular examination, then you should refer to Chapter 6, which describes the purposes and coverage of each examination.

The Business English examinations are more easily classified as they focus on Business or Commercial purposes, from clerical to administrative level. The Study and Training English group cover those examinations which check a person's mastery of English for Study in educational institutions or for practical training purposes in industrial and other work contexts.

The features checklist

As a quick guide to users, the Chart shows which modes are tested, i.e. listening, speaking, reading or writing. All the examining boards listed give their tests in Britain and most also test overseas; this information, plus the frequency of testing, is given in this section of the Chart. Many examinations have special features which distinguish them from the others and these features are also listed.

Further information

To come to a final decision about using a particular examination, users will probably need further detailed information and pointers about how to set about collecting it are given in this final block on the Chart. The reverse side of the Chart will provide some details, the rest of this book and the *Longman Guide to English Language Examinations* will provide more. Direct contact can then be made to individual Boards by getting in touch by post or phone with the addresses given at the bottom of the Chart and in Appendix B.

A few words on using the Chart will be useful here. First, many of the examinations are, in the nature of things, being revised, with new formats and papers due to be introduced as time goes by. Ideas on language teaching and testing change from year to year. New techniques of testing become available as modern technology is introduced. We intend, therefore, to update the Chart at regular intervals. Nevertheless, there will always be the possibility that one or other of the examinations is being phased out and will, before long, be replaced by a new version. In Chapter 6 we will mention any revisions or changes in availability currently being considered by the Boards concerned. Some Boards are willing to hold examinations on demand, or on an Opportunity Basis, arranging the timing and test location to suit the requirements of candidates. Boards making such arrangements usually ask that a reasonable number of candidates are available for such sessions. There are also possibilities of arranging for a Special Mode examination with the content of the test being prepared by local teachers or examiners in agreement with the Board's examiners.

A final comment is about the 'comparability' of the various examinations. Although the ESU levels of the Certificates have been carefully worked out and verified, this does not mean that all certificates at the same level are completely comparable or interchangeable. The purpose of each examination must be carefully examined and the contents checked for relevance to your own purposes. Please refer to Chapter 6 in this book, to the *Longman Guide to English Language Examinations* or to the Boards' own publications. A performance at, say, Level 6 in the Spoken Examination in Social English must, obviously not be equated with a Level 6 performance in Study English. The Chart Levels given, then, must be looked on as a useful introductory guide to what is possible, to be followed by a careful and detailed study of test purpose and content.

Business English

		Pitman	London Chamber of Commerce		
		English for Business Communications	English for Commerce	English for Business	SEFIC
9 Has a full command of the language, with consistent accuracy, fluency, appropriate usage, organisation and comprehension. An exceptional level of mastery, not always reached by native speakers, even quite educated ones.	**9**				
8 Uses a full range of language with proficiency approaching that in the learner's own mother tongue. Copes well even with demanding and complex language situations. Makes occasional minor lapses in accuracy, fluency, appropriacy and organisation which do not affect communication.	**8**				
7 Uses the language fully effectively and confidently in most situations. A few lapses in accuracy, fluency, appropriacy and organisation, but communication is effective and consistent, with only a few uncertainties in conveying or comprehending the content of the message.	**7**	Advanced	Third	Third	Advanced
6 Uses the language with confidence in all but the most demanding situations. Noticeable lapses in accuracy, fluency, appropriacy and organisation, but communication and comprehension are effective on most occasions, and are easily restored when difficulties arise.	**6**	Intermediate	Second	Second	Intermediate
5 Uses the language independently and effectively in all familiar situations. Rather frequent lapses in accuracy, fluency, appropriacy and organisation, but usually succeeds in communicating and comprehending general message.	**5**	Elementary			Threshold
4 Uses a basic range of language, sufficient for familiar and non-pressuring situations. Many lapses in accuracy, fluency, appropriacy and organisation, restricting continual communication and comprehension, so frequent efforts are needed to ensure communicative intention is achieved.	**4**				
3 Uses a limited range of language, sufficient for simple practical needs. In more exacting situations, there are frequent problems in accuracy, fluency, appropriacy and organisation, so that normal communication and comprehension frequently break down or are difficult to keep going.	**3**		First	First	Preliminary
2 Uses a narrow range of language, adequate for basic needs and simple situations. Does not really have sufficient language to cope with normal day-to-day, real-life communication, but basic communication is possible with adequate opportunities for assistance. Uses short, often inaccurately and inappropriately worded messages, with constant lapses in fluency.	**2**				
1 Uses a few words or phrases such as common greetings, and recognises some public notices or signs. At the lowest level, recognises which language is being used.	**1**				

Study/Training English

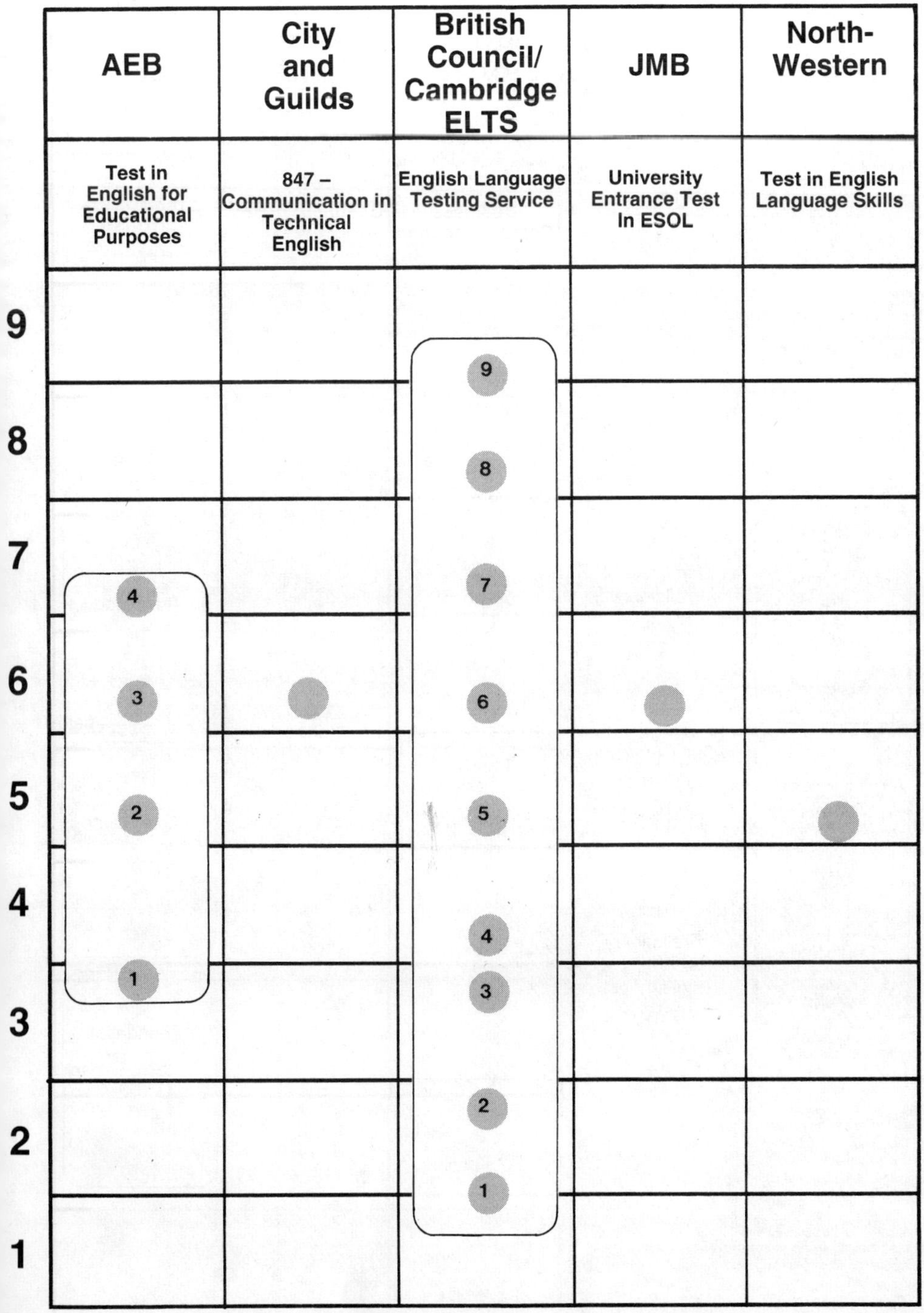

General & Social English

	ARELS	Oxford	Cambridge Syndicate/ RSA		City and Guilds	ESB
	Oral Examinations	Oxford Examinations in EFL	UCLES	CUEFL	361– Communication Skills	Assessments in Spoken English
9						
8	Diploma Pass		Diploma of English Studies			Certificate
7	Higher Certificate Distinction	Distinction Higher Certificate	Pass Certificate of Proficiency	Advanced	III	3 Advanced
6	Credit Pass	Credit Pass	C		II	2 1
5	Very Good Pass	Distinction	First Certificate in English C	Intermediate		3 Intermediate
4	Good Pass Preliminary Certificate	Credit Preliminary Certificate	Preliminary	Basic	I	2 1
3	Pass	Pass	English Test Pass			3 Foundation
2				Foundation		2 1
1						

	Institute of Linguists	University of London		Trinity	NBSD	Pitman
	Examinations in Languages for International Communication	Certificate of Attainment in English	GCE O Level Syllabus B	Spoken English Grades	English as a Foreign Language	English For Speakers of Other Languages
9						
8	Diploma			12		
7	Intermediate Diploma	6		11	7, 6	Advanced
6	Advanced Certificate	5, 4	C	10	Advanced, 5	Higher Intermediate
5		3		9, 8	4	Intermediate
4	General Certificate			7, 6	Intermediate, 3	
3	Preliminary Certificate	2		5, 4	2	Elementary
2		1		3, 2, 1	Elementary, 1	Basic
1						

Chapter 5
The Yardsticks

In this chapter, we present the Yardsticks we have prepared for the Framework examinations. The detailed descriptions of each examination in Chapter 6 will mention those Yardsticks which concern that particular examination. The Yardsticks can be used, not only for assessment purposes, but also for defining learners' needs, textbook design and language programmes (including languages other than English) as you will see in Chapter 9.

The twenty-two Yardsticks in this chapter are presented according to the Five Stages of our model in Figure 5.1 below

Figure 5.1

Yardstick Number		Name
1	Stage I:	Overall language proficiency
2	Stage II:	Oral proficiency
3	Stage II:	Graphic proficiency
4	Stage III:	Listening
5	Stage III:	Speaking
6	Stage III:	Reading
7	Stage III:	Writing
8	Stage IV:	Listening for social and personal purposes
9	Stage IV:	Listening for business purposes
10	Stage IV:	Listening for study/training purposes
11	Stage IV:	Speaking for social and personal purposes
12	Stage IV:	Speaking for business purposes
13	Stage IV:	Speaking for study/training purposes
14	Stage IV:	Reading for social and personal purposes
15	Stage IV:	Reading for business purposes
16	Stage IV:	Reading for study/training purposes
17	Stage IV:	Writing for social and personal purposes
18	Stage IV:	Writing for business purposes
19	Stage IV:	Writing for study/training purposes
20	Stage V:	Linguistic skills
21	Stage V:	Functional skills
22	Stage V:	Examination skills

All Yardsticks have been built up, in a consistent way, out of three elements, namely:

- The ESU Nine Levels.
- A description of task difficulty, or Input.
- A description of expected candidate performance, or Output, according to the handling of the message, the text and the language.

More Yardsticks can be produced, as we suggested in Chapter 2, but we have found the above degree of detail sufficient for most assessors.

YARDSTICK 1
Stage I: Overall language proficiency

9	Has a full command of the language, tackling the most difficult tasks with consistent accuracy, fluency, appropriate usage, organisation and comprehension. An exceptional level of mastery, not always reached by native speakers, even quite educated ones.
8	Uses a full range of language with proficiency approaching that in the learner's own mother tongue. Copes well even with demanding and complex language situations. Makes occasional minor lapses in accuracy, fluency, appropriacy and organisation which do not affect communication. Only rare uncertainties in conveying or comprehending the content of the message.
7	Uses language effectively and in most situations, except the very complex and difficult. A few lapses in accuracy, fluency, appropriacy and organisation, but communication is effective and consistent, with only a few uncertainties in conveying or comprehending the content of the message.
6	Uses the language with confidence in moderately difficult situations. Noticeable lapses in accuracy, fluency, appropriacy and organisation in complex situations, but communication and comprehension are effective on most occasions, and are easily restored when difficulties arise.
5	Uses the language independently and effectively in all familiar and moderately difficult situations. Rather frequent lapses in accuracy, fluency, appropriacy and organisation, but usually succeeds in communicating and comprehending general message.
4	Uses basic range of language, sufficient for familiar and non- pressuring situations. Many lapses in accuracy, fluency, appropriacy and organisation, restricting continual communication and comprehension, so frequent efforts are needed to ensure communicative intention is achieved.
3	Uses a limited range of language, sufficient for simple practical needs. In more exacting situations, there are frequent problems in accuracy, fluency, appropriacy and organisation, so that normal communication and comprehension frequently break down or are difficult to keep going.
2	Uses a very narrow range of language, adequate for basic needs and simple situations. Does not really have sufficient language to cope with normal day-to-day, real-life communication, but basic communication is possible with adequate opportunities for assistance. Uses short, often inaccurately and inappropriately worded messages, with constant lapses in fluency.
1	Uses a few words or phrases such as common greetings, and recognises some public notices or signs. At the lowest level, recognises which language is being used.

YARDSTICK 2
Stage II: Oral proficiency

9	Handles all oral interaction with confidence and competence similar to those in own mother tongue. An exceptional level of oral proficiency. Handles the complete message in oral interaction without undue need for repair. Has complete mastery of text organisation and appropriacy of style. Participates flexibly in interaction conducted at high speed. Handles a complete range of language. Brings a complete command of accuracy to oral interaction. Little L1 accent.
8	Handles a full range of oral interaction with confidence and competence which approach those in own mother tongue. Handles the full message in oral interaction with only occasional loss of detail. Only occasional need for repair. Has a full mastery of text organisation and appropriacy of style. Participates fully and fluently in interaction conducted at speed. Handles a full range of language. Brings a full command of accuracy to the interaction. Residual L1 accent.
7	Handles a wide range of oral interaction with good confidence and competence. Handles the message clearly with only minor loss of detail and little need for repair. Has a wide mastery of text organisation and appropriacy of style. Participates readily in oral interaction but with minor lapses in fluency. Handles a wide range of language. Brings a very good grasp of accuracy to the interaction. Speaks with a noticeable L1 accent.
6	Handles moderate-level oral interaction with good confidence and competence, but with some problems with higher-level interaction. Handles the message adequately but with noticeable loss of detail and need for repair. Has an adequate mastery of text organisation but some uncertainties over appropriacy of style. Some loss of fluency which hampers full participation in oral interaction. Handles a good range of language. Brings a good grasp of accuracy to the interaction. Speaks with marked L1 accent.
5	Handles moderate-level oral interaction with adequate confidence and competence. Handles the major points of the message but with frequent loss of detail. Fairly frequent need for repair. Has a basic mastery of text organisation but an uncertain grasp of style. Limitations restrict participation in oral interaction at times, with fairly frequent lapses in fluency. Handles a moderate range of language. Brings a moderate grasp of accuracy to the interaction. Speaks with obvious L1 accent.
4	Handles simple oral interaction with good confidence and competence, but some problems with moderate-level interaction. Handles the essential points of the message but with great loss of detail. Frequent need for repair. Has frequent problems with text organisation and a limited sensitivity to style. Participates in structured interaction but more restricted in freer interaction. Handles a limited range of language. Brings a limited grasp of accuracy to the interaction. Speaks with a heavy L1 accent.

3	Handles simple oral interaction with adequate confidence and competence, but many problems with moderate-level interaction. Handles the gist of the message; alternatively, handles the needed or predicted items. Constant need for repair. Has little appreciation of text organisation and little grasp of style. Participation in interaction at normal speed is limited, requiring a sympathetic interlocutor. Handles a narrow range of language. Brings a basic level of accuracy to the interaction. Speaks with a very heavy L1 accent.
2	Handles simple oral interaction with erratic confidence and competence. Handles isolated points of the message. Dependent on opportunities for repair to convey or comprehend message. Appreciation of text organisation restricted to sequencing or structured interaction. At the margins of oral communication. Handles a very narrow range of language. Has little grasp of accuracy. L1 accent may make oral communication very limited.
1	Handles only the simplest oral interaction, and that with uncertain confidence and little competence. Handles only the basic or predictable elements of the message. Totally dependent on ample opportunities for repair. Handles texts at the word or phrase level, with organisation limited to the structure of the interaction. Totally dependent on a sympathetic interlocutor. Handles a basic range of language. Has no grasp of accuracy. L1 accent likely to make oral interaction difficult to conduct.

YARDSTICK 3
Stage II: Graphic proficiency

9	Handles all graphic communication with confidence and competence similar to those in own mother tongue. An exceptional level of graphic proficiency. Handles the complete message in graphic communication without undue need for repair. Has complete mastery of text organisation and written style. Flexibly adjusts reading and writing strategies. Reads and writes at high speed. Handles a complete range of language. Brings a complete command of accuracy to graphic communication.
8	Handles a full range of graphic communication with confidence and competence which approach those in own mother tongue. Handles the full message in graphic communication with only occasional loss of detail. Only occasional need for repair. Has full mastery of text organisation and appropriacy of written style. Reads and writes fluently at speed. Handles a full range of language. Brings a full command of accuracy to graphic communication.
7	Handles a wide range of graphic communication with good confidence and competence. Handles the message clearly with only minor loss of detail and little need for repair. Has a wide mastery of text organisation and appropriacy of written style. Reads and writes readily with only minor lapses in fluency. Handles a wide range of language. Brings a very good grasp of accuracy to graphic communication.
6	Handles moderate-level graphic communication with good confidence and competence, but some problems with higher-level communication. Handles the message adequately but with noticeable loss of detail and need for repair. Has an adequate mastery of text organisation but some uncertainties over appropriacy of written style. Some loss of fluency which hampers full participation in graphic communication. Handles a good range of language. Brings a good grasp of accuracy to graphic communication.
5	Handles moderate-level graphic communication with adequate confidence and competence. Handles the major points of the message but with frequent loss of detail. Fairly frequent need for repair. Has a basic mastery of text organisation but an uncertain grasp of written style. Limitations restrict reading and writing activities, with fairly frequent lapses in fluency. Handles a moderate range of language. Brings a moderate grasp of accuracy to graphic communication.
4	Handles simple graphic communication with good confidence and competence, but some problems with moderate-level communication. Handles the essential points of the message but with great loss of detail. Frequent need for repair. Has frequent difficulties with text organisation and limited sensitivity to written style. Reading and writing speed, fluency and flexibility restricted by frequent need to backtrack and refer to a dictionary. Handles a moderate range of language. Brings a limited grasp of accuracy to graphic communication.

3	Handles simple graphic communication with adequate confidence and competence, but many problems with moderate-level communication. Handles the gist of the message; alternatively, handles the needed or predicted items. Constant need for repair. Has little appreciation of text organisation and little grasp of written style. Reading and writing at normal speed are limited, requiring laboured backtracking. Handles a narrow range of language. Brings a basic grasp of accuracy to graphic communication.
2	Handles simple graphic communication with erratic confidence and competence. Handles isolated points of the message. Dependent on opportunities for repair to convey or comprehend the message. Appreciation of text organisation restricted to sequencing. At the margins of graphic communication. Handles a very narrow range of language. Has little grasp of accuracy to bring to graphic communication.
1	Handles the simplest graphic communication and that with uncertain confidence and competence. Handles the basic or predictable elements of the message. Totally dependent on ample opportunities for repair. Handles texts at the word or phrase level. Handles organisation according to the layout of the text (eg. following headings when completing a form). Requires assistance for all but the most basic documents. Graphic communication difficult to conduct at this level. Handles a basic range of language. Has no grasp of accuracy to bring to the text.

YARDSTICK 4
Stage III: Listening

9	Handles all general listening operations, as well as those in own specialist areas,with confidence and competence similar to those in own mother tongue. An exceptional level of listening. Extracts the full content of the message without undue need for repetition or repair. Easily compensates for difficulties and shortcomings in organisation, style, speed of fluency or texts. Listening strategies comparable with those in mother tongue. Handles a complete range of language in listening operations, and compensates easily for distortions and errors.
8	Handles a full range of listening operations with confidence and competence which approach those in own mother tongue. Extracts the full content of the message with only occasional loss of detail or subtlety. Only occasional need for repetition, rephrasing or repair. Only rare uncertainties over organisation, style or fluency of texts. Flexibly adjusts listening strategies to purpose, type and speed of input or interaction. Handles a full range of language, and fully compensates for distortions and errors.
7	Handles a wide range of listening operations with good confidence and competence. Extracts the majority of message with only minor loss of detail or subtlety, and only occasional need for repetition, rephrasing or repair. Few uncertainties over organisation, style or fluency of texts. Strategies fully effective with input delivered at normal speed, but less flexible than in own language. Handles a wide range of language in listening operations, usually with little difficulty in compensating for distortions and errors.
6	Handles moderate listening operations with good confidence and competence but some problems with higher-level operations. Extracts most of the message but with noticeable loss of detail or subtlety. Some need for repetition, rephrasing or repair. Adequately handles organisation, style and fluency of texts. Flexible strategies with input delivered at normal speed, but with some delay for adjustment at first. Handles a fair range of language, often compensating for distortions and errors.
5	Handles moderate-level listening operations with competence and confidence. Extracts major points of message but with frequent loss of detail and subtlety. Fairly frequent need for repetition, rephrasing or repair. Some problems with organisation, style and fluency of texts. Handles straightforward input delivered at normal speed. Employs good strategies when listening with full attention. Handles a moderate range of language, sometimes compensating for distortions or errors.
4	Handles simple listening operations with good confidence and competence, but some problems with moderate-level operations. Extracts essential points of message but with great loss of detail and little grasp of subtlety. Frequent need for repetition, rephrasing or repair. Frequent problems with organisation, style and fluency of texts. Limited ability to handle input at normal speed. Strategies adequate for speech directed at him/her. Handles a limited language range; occasionally compensates for distortions or errors.

3	Handles simple listening operations with adequate competence and confidence but has many problems with moderate-level operations. Comprehends the gist of the message but with little detail and with difficulty in assessing the significance of content. Constant need for repetition and repair. Constant problems with organisation, style and fluency of texts. Greatly limited ability to handle input at normal speed. Requires clear speech directed at him/her. Handles a narrow range of language; unlikely to compensate for distortions or errors.
2	Handles simple listening operations with erratic competence and confidence. Comprehends isolated points of the message or the topic under discussion, often with non-linguistic aid. Dependent on repetition, rephrasing and repair. Little appreciation of organisation or style; mostly listens to very brief texts delivered at reduced speed. Strategies dependent on sympathetic speaker speaking clearly and slowly directly to him/her. Handles a very narrow range of language; unable to compensate for distortions or errors.
1	Handles only the simplest listening operations such as short isolated exchanges (eg. greetings, giving times, prices) and with little confidence. Extracts only basic or predicted messages, or those translated using a dictionary or phrase book. Totally dependent on repetition, rephrasing and repair. At the lowest level, recognises which language is being spoken. No appreciation of organisation or style. Handles texts or interaction at the word or phrase level delivered below normal speed. Strategies limited to clear, slow and repeated speech directed to him/her by sympathetic speaker. Handles a basic range of language; quite unable to compensate for distortions or errors.

YARDSTICK 5

Stage III: Speaking

9	Handles all general speech situations, as well as those in own specialist areas, with confidence and competence similar to those in mother tongue. An exceptional level of speaking. Message required is completely conveyed with total relevance and interest. Message fully adjusted to listener's knowledge of topic and language. Spoken text is coherently organised with suitable use of sequencing and cohesion. Total control of fluency in interaction without undue hesitations. Style effectively matched to context. Language control complete, allowing for high-level interaction. Complete accuracy apart from occasional 'slips of tongue'. Little L1 accent and appropriate use of idiom contribute to overall impression.
8	Handles a full range of speech situations with confidence and competence approaching that in L1. Message required is effectively conveyed, with interesting and attractive treatment of topic. Message well adjusted to listener's knowledge of topic and language. Spoken text is well organised with good sequencing and cohesion. Conversation well sustained. Style well adjusted to context. Fluency is good with few false starts or hesitations. Language repertoire good, with few 'slips of the tongue'. Residual L1 accent but pronunciation, intonation and stress patterns all assist communication.
7	Handles a wide range of speech operations with good confidence and competence. Message is clearly conveyed and with interest. Presentation and interaction relevant and appropriate to listener's knowledge of topic and language. Spoken text is clearly organised with suitable sequencing and cohesion. Occasionally lacks fluency and flexibility, with some lapses of appropriacy and linguistic uncertainty. Uses coping strategies effectively. Uses a wide language repertoire with occasional lapses of accuracy. Speech features influenced by L1 but these in no way affect communication.
6	Handles moderate-level speech situations with good confidence and competence, but some problems with higher-level situations. Message adequately conveyed. Basic communication is adequate but some restrictions in participation because of language limitations. Spoken text is adequately organised but with some lapses in sequencing and cohesion. Some sense of appropriate style. Noticeable false starts, hesitations and reformulations. Uses a fair language repertoire. Accuracy and usage good in spite of noticeable lapses. Marked L1 speech features but these rarely affect essential communication.
5	Handles moderate speech situations with adequate confidence and competence. Message is broadly conveyed but with little subtlety and some loss of detail. Some difficulties in initiating and sustaining conversation. Interaction needs repetition and clarification. Spoken text organisation is adequate but with fairly frequent stylistic lapses. Fairly frequent hesitations and lapses in fluency, but these do not interfere with basic communication. Uses a moderate language repertoire, but has to search for words and use circumlocutions. Fairly frequent errors in accuracy. Obvious L1 accent and speech features. Limitations impair communication at times.

4	Handles simple speech situations with good confidence and competence, but some problems with moderate-level situations. Conveys short, simple messages but with loss of detail and interest. Frequent need for repetition and clarification. Responds adequately to structured conversation but restricted in freer interaction. Spoken text organisation is haphazard and lapses require frequent repair. Little stylistic variation. Communication adequately conveys the speaker's gist. Frequent false starts and hesitations. Uses a limited language repertoire with little variety. Frequent errors. Heavy L1 accent. Language limitations impede intelligibility
3	Handles simple speech situations with adequate confidence and competence, but many problems with moderate-level situations. Conveys basic survival messages, but lacks clarity and interest. Communication breaks down as language constraints interfere with message. Little text organisation or flexibility of response. Little appreciation of style. Restricted to handling basic facts. False starts and hesitations impair communication. Has a narrow language repertoire, demanding constant rephrasing and searching for words. Errors even with quite basic usage. Pronunciation and usage shortcomings cause very frequent problems with communication.
2	Handles simple speech situations with erratic confidence and competence. Conveys the shortest, simplest and most factual aspects of the message. Responses often irrelevant. At the margins of communication. Spoken text organisation restricted to responses to predictable gambits or expressing basic needs. Sympathetic interlocutor is needed to maintain communication. No stylistic variation. Has a very narrow language repertoire of isolated words and phrases. Language inaccuracies and pronunciation shortcomings make spoken communication quite difficult.
1	Handles only the simplest speech situations, eg. giving name, nationality, etc in structured situations. Any message is difficult to decipher; or at the lowest level, not enough evidence to assess proficiency. Produces spoken texts which are little more than a string of words or groups of words without coherence. Little or no proficiency in dialogue. At the lowest level, unable to take part in dialogue, providing inadequate speech for proper assessment. Has only the most basic language repertoire, with little or no evidence of a functional command of the language. L1 speech features and limited language make speech very difficult to comprehend.

YARDSTICK 6
Stage III: Reading

9	Reads all general texts and texts in own specialist areas with confidence and competence similar to those in mother tongue. An exceptional level of reading. Comprehends full content of message without the need for a dictionary. Easily compensates for difficulties or shortcomings in organisation, style or fluency of texts. Reading speeds and strategies comparable with those in mother tongue. Handles a complete range of language in reading texts, and compensates easily for misprints and errors.
8	Reads a full range of texts with competence and confidence approaching those in mother tongue. Comprehends the full content of message with only occasional loss of detail or subtlety, and only occasional use of a dictionary. Only rare uncertainties over organisation, style or fluency of texts. Flexibly adapts reading speed and strategies to reading purpose and type of text. Handles a full range of language, fully compensating for misprints and errors.
7	Reads a wide range of reading texts with good confidence and competence. Comprehends the majority of the message with only minor loss of detail or subtlety. Little need to refer to a dictionary. Few uncertainties over the organisation, style or fluency of texts. Reading speed and strategies fully effective but somewhat less flexible than those in own language. Handles a wide range of language, usually with little trouble compensating for misprints and errors.
6	Reads moderate-level texts with good confidence and competence, but some problems with higher-level texts. Comprehends most of the message but with noticeable loss of detail and subtlety. Some need to refer to a dictionary. Adequately handles organisation, style or fluency of texts. Good reading speed and flexible reading strategies. Handles a fair range of language, often compensating for misprints and errors.
5	Reads moderate-level texts with adequate competence and confidence. Comprehends major points of the message but with frequent loss of detail or subtlety. Fairly frequent need to refer to a dictionary. Some problems with organisation, style and fluency of texts. Good reading speed of straightforward texts. Handles a moderate range of language, sometimes compensating for misprints and errors.
4	Reads simple texts with good competence and confidence, but some problems with moderate-level texts. Comprehends essential points of message but with great loss of detail and little concept of subtlety. Frequent need to refer to a dictionary. Frequent problems with organisation, style and fluency of texts. Reading speed and flexibility restricted by frequent need to re-read or refer to dictionary. Handles a limited range of language, occasionally compensating for misprints and errors.

3	Reads simple texts with adequate competence and confidence, but has many problems with moderate-level texts. Comprehends the gist of the message but with little detail and with difficulty in assessing the significance of information. Constant need to refer to a dictionary. Constant problems with organisation, style and fluency of texts. Reads slowly. Handles a narrow range of language. Unlikely to compensate for misprints or errors.
2	Reads simple texts with erratic competence and confidence. Comprehends isolated points of message or the topic under discussion, often with non-linguistic aid. Dependent on a dictionary. Little appreciation of organisational devices or style; mostly reads texts at sentence level. Reads very slowly. Handles a very narrow range of language. No ability to compensate for misprints or errors.
1	Reads only the simplest texts such as public notices or signs. Comprehends only basic and common messages, or those translated with the aid of a bilingual dictionary. At the lowest level, recognises which language is written. No appreciation of organisational devices or style. Reads texts mostly below sentence level. Reads extremely slowly. Handles a basic range of language. Unlikely to recognise misprints or errors.

YARDSTICK 7
Stage III: Writing

9	Writes all general texts and texts in own specialist areas with confidence and competence similar to those in mother tongue. An exceptional level of writing. Message is completely conveyed with total relevance and interest. Message fully adjusted to reader's knowledge of topic and language. Text is coherently organised with effective use of cohesive devices. Layout and structure aid force of argument. Style effectively matched to topic and reader. Language control complete apart from occasional obvious 'slips'. Complete accuracy, fluency and appropriate use of idiom contribute to overall impression of writing.
8	Writes a full range of texts with competence and confidence approaching those in L1. Message required is effectively conveyed, with interesting and attractive treatment of topic. Length matches requirements of task. Message well adjusted to reader. Text organisation is clear with appropriate cohesive devices. Style suits subject. Good sentence variety. Text flows. Layout and punctuation helpful. Language repertoire good. Correct and appropriate usage of grammar and vocabulary. Few formal errors apart from 'slips'. Spelling and writing help intelligibility.
7	Writes a wide range of texts with good confidence and competence. Message is clearly conveyed. Interesting treatment. Suitable length. Presentation relevant to task and reader. Text accurately presented with clarity of organisation with suitable use of cohesion and topic markers. Style well adjusted to task. Layout and punctuation helpful. Uses a wide language repertoire accurately, with occasional lapses of appropriacy and inaccuracies. Spelling and handwriting good.
6	Writes moderate-level texts with good confidence and competence, but some problems with higher-level texts. Message adequately conveyed. Basic ideas conveyed with clarity and relevance to reader. Language limitations impede fully effective performance. Text is adequately presented but with lapses in flow, organisation and cohesion. Has a limited stylistic range. Punctuation and layout basically helpful. Has fair language repertoire but with several lapses in accuracy. Idiom, if used at all, may be unsuitable. Spelling and handwriting quite clear and intelligible.
5	Writes moderate-level texts with adequate competence and confidence. Message is broadly conveyed but with little subtlety. Often bald and halting, reducing interest. Reader has to backtrack on occasion to clarify thread of topic. Text organisation adequate but presentation lacks subtlety. Some use of stylistic variation and basic cohesive devices. Punctuation and layout acceptable. Has a moderate language repertoire, but fairly frequent errors and inappropriacies. Meaning of sentences conveyed. Spelling and handwriting legible.

4	Writes simple texts with good competence and confidence; some problems with moderate-level texts. Message conveyed basically but without subtlety. Deals with main topic required but with lack of clarity and interest. Marginally communicative. Text organisation haphazard and not coherent throughout. Little use of stylistic variation or cohesive devices. Punctuation, paragraphing and layout basic. Uses a limited language repertoire with little variety and frequent inaccuracies. Spelling and handwriting impede clarity of message.
3	Writes simple texts with adequate competence and confidence, but with many problems with moderate-level texts. Produces a string of sentences bearing to some extent on the required message. Little sense of reader expectations. Finer details not dealt with. Lacking in interest. Little sense of text organisation. Mainly descriptive or narrative style lacking cohesion. Punctuation basic and often omitted. Layout of little help to reader. Has a narrow language repertoire, with regular inaccuracies and inappropriacies which impede basic message. Spelling and handwriting cause problems of intelligibility.
2	Writes simple texts with erratic competence and confidence. Manages a few simple sentences, but relationship to required message is tenuous. Little intrinsic interest. Subsidiary themes and details ignored or presented in confused ways. Little text organisation with little cohesion between its sentences. Lacks flow. No stylistic variation. Punctuation and layout not helpful to reader. Has a very narrow language repertoire, with many inaccuracies. Spelling errors and poor handwriting make topic rather difficult to discern.
1	Writes only the simplest texts, eg. completing forms with name, address, etc. Any message is difficult to decipher; or not enough evidence to assess proficiency. Produces texts which are little more than a string of words or groups of words without coherence; or does not provide enough evidence to assess properly. Has only the most basic language repertoire, with little or no evidence of a functional grasp of lexis or sentence structure. Handwriting and spelling may make text very difficult to read.

YARDSTICK 8
Stage IV: Listening for social and personal purposes

Typical tasks: Listening to public announcements, lectures/talks for personal interest, radio/television programmes, personal/social telephone calls, etc.

9	Handles all social/personal listening operations in areas of own and related interests with confidence and competence similar to those in mother tongue. An exceptional level of social listening. Extracts the complete message from social/personal texts without undue need for repair. Skilfully processes and evaluates the message for subsequent application. Easily handles extended or complex texts such as broadcasts, lectures/talks or telephone calls delivered at high speed. Social listening strategies comparable with those in mother tongue. Handles a complete range of social language in own and a broad range of related interests. Compensates easily for distortions or errors in transmitted and live texts of a social/personal nature.
8	Handles a full range of social/personal listening operations with confidence and competence which approach those in own mother tongue. Extracts the full message from announcements, broadcasts, talks, etc. with only occasional loss of detail or subtlety. Uses a full range of techniques to evaluate, apply or relay the message. Flexibly adjusts listening strategies to long and detailed social/personal texts delivered at speed. Handles a full range of social language in own and related areas of interest. Compensates fully for distortions in transmitted or live texts of a social/personal nature.
7	Handles a wide range of social/personal listening operations, with good confidence and competence. Extracts the majority of the message from announcements, broadcasts, talks, etc. with only minor loss of detail or subtlety. Uses a good range of techniques to evaluate, apply or relay the message. Listening strategies fully effective for dealing with social/personal texts delivered at normal speed, but less flexible than in mother tongue. Handles a wide range of social language in own and related areas of interest. Little difficulty in compensating for distortions and errors in transmitted or live texts of a social/personal nature.
6	Handles moderate-level social/personal listening operations with fair confidence and competence, but some difficulties with higher-level operations, especially if opportunities for repair are limited. Extracts most of the message from announcements, broadcasts, talks, etc. but with noticeable loss of detail and subtlety. Uses a good range of techniques to store and apply or relay the message. Uses flexible strategies for social/personal texts delivered at normal speed, but with problems of initial adjustment to style, accent, and speed or mode of delivery. Handles a good range of social language in areas of general and own particular interests. Usually compensates for distortions and errors in transmitted or live texts of a social/personal nature.
5	Handles moderate-level social/personal listening operations with confidence and competence. Extracts the major points of the message from announcements, broadcasts, talks, etc. but with frequent loss of detail and subtlety. Uses a fair

	range of techniques to store and apply or relay the message. Handles straightforward social/personal texts in areas of own interests or need if delivered at normal speed and if listening with full attention. Handles a moderate range of social language in areas of general and own particular interests. Sometimes compensates for distortions and errors in transmitted or live texts of a social/personal nature.
4	Handles simple social/personal listening operations with confidence and competence, but some limitations on moderate-level operations, especially if few or no opportunities for repair. Extracts the broad outline of the message from announcements, broadcasts, talks, etc. but with great loss of detail and subtlety. Uses a limited range of techniques to store, apply or relay the message. Limited ability to handle social/personal texts in areas of own interests or needs when delivered at normal speed, unless directed specifically at him/her, eg. personal or predictable messages. Handles a limited range of social language relating to own particular interests. Occasionally compensates for distortions or errors in live texts of a social/personal nature.
3	Handles simple social/personal listening operations with adequate confidence and competence, but has many problems with moderate-level operations, especially if there are limited opportunities for repair. Comprehends the gist of the message of a broadcast or talk, but with little detail; alternatively extracts needed or predicted items of isolated information from announcements or broadcasts. Greatly limited ability to handle social/personal texts delivered at normal speed. Requires clear speech specifically relevant to him/her, with opportunities for repair or repetition. Handles a narrow range of social language in areas relating to own particular needs or interests. Unlikely to compensate for distortions or errors in transmitted or live texts of a social/personal nature.
2	Handles simple social/personal listening operations with erratic confidence and competence. Comprehends isolated points of the message and can identify the topic of a talk or broadcast. Further comprehension depends on L1 or visual support or demonstration. Stores basic factual information, eg. prices, times, platform or gate numbers, temperatures, etc. Mostly handles very brief social/personal texts delivered at reduced speed or repeated. Requires sympathetic speaker who will speak slowly and clearly, and repeat or reformulate. Handles a very narrow range of social language in areas relating to own particular needs or interests. Unable to compensate for distortions or errors in transmitted or live texts of a social/personal nature.
1	Handles the simplest social/personal listening operations such as isolated or predictable announcements with little confidence, especially if few opportunities for repair. Identifies topic or basic message of an announcement or broadcast. Further comprehension requires translation or visuals. Ability to store or relay message limited by level of comprehension. Handles the briefest social/personal texts, such as airport announcements or recorded telephone messages. Requires slow, clear and repeated speech. Has small range of social language - international terms: taxi, telephone, etc. Quite unable to compensate for distortions or errors in social listening texts.

YARDSTICK 9

Stage IV: Listening for business purposes

Typical tasks: Taking business telephone messages, listening to business meetings, conferences or presentations, etc.

9	Handles all business listening operations in own and in related areas of responsibility with confidence and competence similar to those in mother tongue. An exceptional level of business listening. Extracts the complete message of a business call, meetings or presentation without undue need for repair. Uses a comprehensive range of techniques to store or relay the message for later business applications. Easily handles extended or complex business texts such as telephone calls, meetings or presentations delivered at high speed. Business listening strategies comparable with those in mother tongue. Handles a complete range of business language and specialist terminology in own and a broad range of related fields. Easily compensates for distortions and errors in business listening texts.
8	Handles a full range of business listening operations with confidence and competence which approach those in own mother tongue. Extracts the full message of a business call, meeting or presentation with only occasional loss of detail or subtlety. Uses a full range of techniques to store or relay the message for later applications. Flexibly adjusts listening strategies to long and detailed business texts delivered at speed. Handles a full range of business language and specialist terminology in own and related fields. Fully compensates for distortions and errors in business listening texts.
7	Handles a wide range of business listening operations with good confidence and competence. Extracts the majority of the message of a business call or meeting with only minor loss of detail or subtlety. Uses a good range of techniques to store or relay the message for later business applications. Listening strategies fully effective for dealing with business texts such as telephone calls, meetings or presentations delivered at normal speed, but less flexible than in own mother tongue. Handles a wide range of business language and specialist terminology in own and related fields. Little difficulty in compensating for distortions and errors in business listening texts.
6	Handles moderate-level business listening operations with confidence and competence, but some difficulties with higher-level operations, especially if opportunities for repair are limited. Extracts most of the message of a business call, meeting or presentation, but with noticeable loss of detail or subtlety. Uses a good range of techniques to store or relay the message for later application. Uses flexible strategies for business texts delivered at normal speed, but with problems of initial adjustment to style, accent or speed of delivery. Handles a good range of business language and specialist terminology in own field. Usually compensates for distortions and errors in business listening texts.

5	Handles moderate-level listening operations with confidence and competence. Extracts the major points of the message in a business call, meeting or presentation, but with frequent loss of detail or subtlety. Uses a fair range of techniques to store or relay the message for later business applications. Handles straightforward business texts in own field delivered at normal speed when listening with full attention. Handles a moderate range of business language and specialist terminology in own field. Sometimes compensates for errors in business listening texts.
4	Handles simple business listening operations with good confidence and competence, but some limitations on moderate-level operations, especially if limited opportunities for repair. Extracts the broad outline of the message in a business call or presentation, but with great loss of detail and subtlety. Uses a limited range of techniques to store or relay the message. Limited ability to handle business texts in own field delivered at normal speed, unless directed specifically at him/her, eg. one-to-one telephone calls. Handles a limited range of business language relating directly to own field. Occasionally compensates for errors in business listening texts.
3	Handles simple business listening operations with some confidence and competence, but has many problems with moderate-level operations, especially if limited opportunities for repair. Comprehends gist of a message or extracts information needed. Takes brief notes (probably in L1) but with missing information and difficulty in assessing the significance of the content for later business applications. Greatly limited ability to handle business texts delivered at normal speed. Requires clear speech directed specifically at him/her, with opportunities for repair. Handles a narrow range of business language and the most common specialist terms in own field. Unlikely to compensate for distortions.
2	Handles simple business listening operations with erratic confidence and competence. Comprehends isolated points of the business message and can identify the topic of a call, meeting or presentation. Further comprehension depends on L1 support or visual aids and demonstrations. Takes simple notes in L1 of basic factual or numerical information. Mostly handles very brief business texts delivered at reduced speed. Requires sympathetic speaker speaking clearly and slowly. Handles a very narrow range of business language and a few specialist terms. Unable to compensate for distortions or errors in business listening texts.
1	Handles the simplest business listening operations, such as isolated exchanges or instructions. Handles these with uncertain confidence or competence, especially if there aren't extensive repair opportunities. Identifies the topic or basic message of a call or meeting. Further comprehension requires translation, accompanying visual aids or demonstration. Ability to relay message restricted by level of comprehension. Handles the briefest business texts, such as recorded telephone services (eg. exchange rates). Requires slow, clear speech and repeated listening. Handles a basic range of business language such as terms similar to those in L1. Quite unable to compensate for distortions or errors in business listening texts.

YARDSTICK 10

Stage IV: Listening for study/training purposes

Typical tasks: Listening to lectures, academic discussions, broadcasts on academic topics, workshop demonstrations, training presentations, practical instructions, etc.

9	Handles all study/training listening operations in own and related specialist fields with confidence and competence similar to those in own mother tongue. An exceptional level of study listening. Extracts the complete message of a lecture or training presentation without undue need for repair. Uses a comprehensive range of note-taking and retrieval techniques for later study applications. Easily handles extended and complex study/training texts such as lectures or presentations delivered at high speed. Academic listening strategies comparable to those in mother tongue. Handles a complete range of academic language conventions and specialist terminology in own and a broad range of related fields. Compensates easily for distortions in lecture delivery or training sessions.
8	Handles a full range of study/training listening operations with confidence and competence which approach those in own mother tongue. Extracts the full message of a lecture or training presentation with only occasional loss of detail or subtlety. Uses a full range of note-taking and retrieval techniques for later study applications. Flexibly adjusts listening strategies to long and detailed study/training texts delivered at speed. Handles a full range of academic language and specialist terminology in own and related specialist fields. Fully compensates for distortions and errors in lectures or training presentations.
7	Handles a wide range of study/training listening operations with good confidence and competence. Extracts the majority of the message of a lecture or training presentation with only minor loss of detail or subtlety. Uses a wide range of note-taking and retrieval techniques for later applications. Listening strategies fully effective with study/training texts such as lectures or training sessions delivered at normal speed. Handles a wide range of academic language and specialist terminology in own and related fields. Little difficulty in compensating for distortions or errors in lectures or training presentations.
6	Handles moderate-level study/training listening operations with confidence and competence, but some difficulties with higher-level operations, especially if opportunities for repair are limited. Extracts most of the message of a lecture or training presentation, but with noticeable loss of detail and subtlety. Uses a good range of note-taking techniques for later study applications. Uses flexible strategies for study/training texts delivered at normal speed, but with problems of initial adjustment to style, accent, and speed or mode of delivery. Handles a good range of academic language and specialist terminology in own field. Usually compensates for distortions and errors in lectures or training presentations.
5	Handles moderate-level study/training listening operations with confidence and competence. Extracts the major points of the message of a lecture or training presentation, but with frequent loss of detail or subtlety. Uses a fair range of note-taking and retrieval techniques for later study applications. Handles straightforward study/training texts in own field delivered at normal speed when

	listening with full attention. Handles a moderate range of academic language and specialist terminology in own field. Sometimes compensates for distortions and errors in lecture delivery or training presentations.
4	Handles simple study/training listening operations with good confidence and competence, but some limitations on moderate-level operations, especially if there are few or no opportunities for repair. Extracts the broad outline of the message of a lecture or training presentation, but with great loss of detail and subtlety. Uses a limited range of note-taking techniques for later study applications. Limited ability to handle study/training texts in own field delivered at normal speed, unless these are directed specifically at him/her, eg. personal tuition or supervision. Handles a limited range of academic language and specialist terminology relating directly to own field. Occasionally compensates for distortions and errors in lectures or training presentations.
3	Handles simple study/training listening operations with adequate confidence and competence but has many problems with moderate-level operations, especially if there are limited opportunities for repair. Comprehends the gist of the message of academic lectures or training presentations, but with little detail. Takes brief notes (probably in L1) but with missing information and with little reflection of the structure of the original listening text. Greatly limited ability to handle study/training texts delivered at normal speed. Requires clear speech directed specifically at him/her, with opportunities for repair and repetition. Handles a narrow range of academic language and common specialist terms in own field. Unlikely to compensate for distortions in text.
2	Handles simple study/training listening operations with erratic confidence and competence. Comprehends isolated points of the message and can identify the topic of the lecture or training presentation. Further comprehension depends on support from an L1 abstract, visual aids, or an accompanying demonstration. Takes notes in L1 on basic factual or numerical information. Mostly handles very brief training texts delivered at reduced speed. Requires sympathetic trainer speaking clearly and slowly. Handles a very narrow range of academic language and a few specialist terms. Unable to compensate for distortions or errors in study/training presentations.
1	Handles the simplest study/training listening operations such as isolated instructions. Handles these with little confidence and uncertain competence, especially if there aren't extensive repair opportunities. Identifies the topic or basic message of training or instructions. Further comprehension requires translation or accompanying visual aids and demonstration. Note-taking restricted by level of comprehension. Handles the briefest training texts, such as isolated instructions, comments accompanying a demonstration, or terms relating to equipment or operations. Requires slow, clear and repeated instructions. Handles a basic range of specialist language such as terms similar to those in L1. Quite unable to compensate for errors or distortions.

YARDSTICK 11

Stage IV: Speaking for social and personal purposes

Typical tasks: Speaking to give and obtain information, advice, assistance or service (eg travelling), express opinions, to establish social relationships; making social and personal telephone calls; giving talks/broadcasts of personal interest, etc.

9	Handles all social/personal speech situations in areas of own and related interests with confidence and competence similar to those in own mother tongue. An exceptional level of social speaking. Social/personal message is completely conveyed with total relevance and effect. Message completely adjusted to listeners' knowledge of topic, context and language. Social/personal texts such as extended, complex or delicate talks, interaction or telephone calls are coherently organised. No undue hesitations. Style completely adjusted to context and purpose. Controls a complete range of social language in own and a broad range of related interests. Little L1 accent and no intrusive errors of usage.
8	Handles a full range of social/personal speech situations with confidence and competence which approach those in own mother tongue. Social/personal message is fully conveyed, with interest and effect. Message is fully adjusted to listeners' knowledge of topic, context and language. Social/personal texts such as long and detailed talks, interaction or telephone calls are well organised and sustained. Style well adjusted to context and purpose. Fluency is good with few hesitations. Controls a full range of social language in own and related areas of interest. Residual L1 accent and only minor errors of usage.
7	Handles a wide range of social/personal speech situations with good confidence and competence. Social/personal message is clearly conveyed, with interest and effect. Message is well adjusted to listeners' knowledge of topic, context and language. Social/personal texts such as talks, interaction or telephone calls are clearly organised. Occasional lapses in fluency and flexibility, with some uncertainties of appropriacy in style. Controls a wide range of social language in own and related areas of interest. Speech features influenced by L1 and with occasional errors of usage, but these in no way reduce communicative effect.
6	Handles moderate-level social/personal speech situations with good confidence and competence, but some difficulties with higher-level situations. Social/personal message is adequately conveyed. Message is adequately adjusted to listeners' knowledge of topic, context and language. Some restrictions in conversation because of language limitations. Social/personal texts such as talks, interaction and telephone calls are adequately organised but with some lapses in cohesion. Some sense of style suitable to context and purpose. Noticeable lapses in fluency. Controls a good range of social language in areas of general and own particular interests. Marked L1 speech features and noticeable errors of usage, but these rarely affect communication.
5	Handles moderate-level social/personal speech situations with adequate confidence and competence. Social/personal message is broadly conveyed but with little subtlety and some loss of detail. Some limitations in initiating

	conversation and discussion. Message needs repetition and clarification. Social/personal texts such as straightforward talks and discussions are adequately organised. Fairly frequent lapses in style and fluency but these do not interfere with basic communication. Controls a moderate range of social language in areas of general and own particular interests. Fairly frequent errors in usage and obvious L1 speech features impair communication at times.
4	Handles simple social/personal speech situations with good confidence and competence, but some limitations on moderate-level situations. Conveys short, simple social/personal messages but with loss of detail and effect. Frequent need to repeat and rephrase. Restricted participation in freer interaction and telephone conversations. Social/personal text organisation is haphazard and requires frequent repair. Little variation in style or sense of appropriacy to context, purpose or audience. Frequent false starts and hesitations. Controls a limited range of social language relating to own particular needs and interests. Heavy L1 accent and frequent errors of usage impede intelligibility.
3	Handles simple social/personal speech situations with adequate confidence and competence, but many problems with moderate-level situations. Conveys the basic social/personal message but with little detail or clarity. Communication breaks down as language constraints interfere with message. Makes basic contributions to conversation or discussion. Little organisation in social/personal texts. Little appreciation of style or appropriacy. Restricted handling of basic facts and opinions. False starts and hesitations impair social communication. Has a narrow range of social language in areas relating to own particular needs or interests. Shortcomings in basic usage and pronunciation cause very frequent problems in social communication.
2	Handles simple social/personal speech situations with erratic confidence and competence. Conveys the shortest, simplest and most factual aspects of the social/personal message, eg times, prices, personal data, name, address, passport and other numbers, etc. At the margins of social communication. Constant need to repeat and rephrase, needing help from sympathetic listener. Social/personal text organisation is restricted to responding to predictable questions and expressing basic factual information. Sympathetic listener is needed to maintain communication. No appreciation of style. Has a very narrow range of social language relating to own particular needs or interests. Shortcomings in basic usage and pronunciation make social communication very limited.
1	Handles only the simplest social/personal speech situations, eg responding to structured questions in familiar situations. Handles these with uncertain confidence and little competence. Any social/personal message is difficult to comprehend. Produces social/personal texts restricted to groups of words or responses to predictable questions. Has a basic range of social language such as international terms similar to those in L1 (eg hotel, airport, etc.). L1 speech features and limited language make social communication difficult to conduct.

YARDSTICK 12
Stage IV: Speaking for business purposes

Typical tasks: Making business telephone calls; speaking at business meetings and conferences; making business presentations; negotiating business agreements; taking part in job interviews, etc.

9	Handles all business speech situations in own and related areas of responsibility with confidence and competence similar to those in own mother tongue. An exceptional level of business speaking. Business message is completely conveyed with total relevance and effect. Presentation is completely adjusted to listeners' knowledge of topic and language. Business texts such as extended and complex presentations, negotiations or telephone calls are coherently organised. Total control of fluency with no undue hesitations. Style completely adjusted to context. Controls a complete range of business language and specialist terminology in own and a broad range of related fields. Little L1 accent and no intrusive errors of usage.
8	Handles a full range of business speech situations with confidence and competence which approach those in own mother tongue. Business message is fully conveyed, with interest and effect. Presentation is fully adjusted to listeners' knowledge or topic and language. Business texts such as long and detailed presentations, meetings or telephone calls are well organised and sustained. Style well adjusted to context and purpose. Fluency is good with few hesitations. Controls a full range of business language and specialist terminology in own and related fields. Residual L1 accent and only minor errors of usage.
7	Handles a wide range of business speech situations with good confidence and competence. Business message is clearly delivered and with effect. Presentation is well adjusted to listeners' knowledge of topic and language. Business texts such as presentations, meetings and telephone calls are clearly organised. Occasional lapses in fluency and flexibility, with some uncertainties of appropriacy in style. Controls a wide range of business language and specialist terminology in own and related fields. Speech features influenced by L1 and with occasional errors of usage, but these in no way reduce communicative effect.
6	Handles moderate-level business speech situations with good confidence and competence, but some difficulties with higher-level situations. Business message is adequately conveyed. Presentation is adequately adjusted to listeners' knowledge of topic and language. Some restrictions in business discussions because of language limitations. Business texts such as meetings, presentations and telephone calls are adequately organised but with some lapses in cohesion. Some sense of style suitable to context and purpose. Noticeable lapses in fluency. Controls a good range of business language and specialist terminology in own field. Marked L1 speech features and noticeable errors of usage, but these rarely reduce communicative effect.

5	Handles moderate-level business speech situations with adequate confidence and competence. Business message is broadly conveyed but with little subtlety and some loss of detail. Some limitations in initiating and sustaining discussion and negotiation. Presentation needs repetition and clarification. Business texts such as straightforward presentations and discussions adequately organised. Fairly frequent lapses in style and fluency but these do not interfere with basic communication. Controls a moderate range of business language and specialist terminology in own field. Fairly frequent errors in usage and obvious L1 speech features impair communication at times.
4	Handles simple business speech situations with good confidence and competence, but some limitations on moderate-level situations. Conveys short, simple business messages but with loss of detail and effect. Frequent need to repeat and rephrase. Restricted participation in freer business discussions and telephone conversations. Business text organisation is haphazard and requires frequent repair. Little variation in style or sense of appropriacy. Frequent false starts and hesitations. Controls a limited range of business language and specialist terminology in own field. Heavy L1 accent and frequent errors of usage impede intelligibility.
3	Handles simple business speech situations with adequate confidence and competence, but many problems with moderate-level situations. Conveys the basic business message but with little detail or clarity. Communication breaks down as language constraints interfere with message. Makes basic contributions to meetings or discussions. Little organisation in business texts. Little appreciation of style or appropriacy. Restricted to handling basic facts. False starts and hesitations impair communication in business. Has a narrow range of business language and the most common specialist terms in own field. Shortcomings in basic usage and pronunciation cause very frequent problems in conducting business.
2	Handles simple business speech situations with erratic confidence and competence. Conveys the shortest, simplest and most factual aspects of the business message, such as basic arrangements, eg prices, times, dates, places, destinations, names, quantities, etc. At the margins of business communication. Constant false starts, hesitations, repetitions and rephrasing. Business text organisation is restricted to responding to predictable questions and expressing basic factual information. Sympathetic listener is needed to maintain communication. No appreciation of style. Has a very narrow range of business language and a few specialist terms. Shortcomings in basic usage and pronunciation make business in the spoken mode very limited.
1	Handles only the simplest business speech situations, eg responses to structured enquiries requiring factual replies at the word or group-of-word level. Handles these with uncertain confidence and little competence. Any business message is difficult to comprehend. Produces business texts restricted to groups of words or responses to predictable questions. Has a basic range of specialist language such as terms similar to those in L1. L1 speech features and limited language make business in the spoken mode very difficult to conduct or comprehend.

YARDSTICK 13
Stage IV: Speaking for study/training purposes

Typical tasks: Giving a lecture or training presentation; contributing to seminars, discussions, tutorials or training sessions; consultations with supervisors, etc.

9	Handles all study/training speech situations in own and related specialist fields with confidence and competence similar to those in own mother tongue. An exceptional level of study/training speaking. Study/training message is completely conveyed with total relevance and high interest. Presentation is completely adjusted to students'/trainees' knowledge of topic and language. Full use of visual aids. Study/training texts such as extended and complex lectures and demonstrations are coherently organised. Total control of fluency without any undue hesitations. Style completely adjusted to context. Controls a complete range of academic language and specialist terminology in own and a broad range of related fields. Little L1 accent and no intrusive errors of usage.
8	Handles a full range of study/training speech situations with confidence and competence which approach those in own mother tongue. Study/training message is fully conveyed, with interesting and attractive treatment. Presentation is fully adjusted to students'/trainees' knowledge of topic and language. Full use of visual aids. Study/training texts such as long and detailed lectures or demonstrations are well organised and sustained. Style well adjusted to context and purpose. Fluency is good with few hesitations. Controls a full range of academic language and specialist terminology in own and related fields. Residual L1 accent and only minor errors of usage in delivery.
7	Handles a wide range of study/training speech situations with good confidence and competence. Study/training message is clearly delivered and with interest. Presentation is well adjusted to students'/trainees' knowledge of topic and language. Uses a wide range of visual aids. Study/training texts such as lectures, demonstrations and discussions are clearly organised. Occasional lack of fluency and flexibility, with some uncertainties of appropriacy. Controls a wide range of academic language and specialist terminology in own and related fields. Speech features influenced by L1 and with occasional errors of usage, but these in no way reduce communicative effect of delivery.
6	Handles moderate-level study/training speech situations with good confidence and competence, but some difficulties with high-level situations. Study/training message is adequately conveyed. Basic communication is adequate but some restrictions in discussion because of language limitations. Presentation adequately adjusted to trainees' knowledge. Study/training texts such as lectures, demonstrations and discussions are adequately organised but with some lapses in cohesion. Some sense of academic style. Noticeable lapses in fluency. Controls a good range of academic language and specialist terminology in own field. Marked L1 speech features and noticeable errors of usage, but these rarely reduce communicative effect.

5	Handles moderate-level study/training speech situations with adequate confidence and competence. Study/training message is broadly conveyed but with little subtlety and some loss of detail. Some limitations in initiating and sustaining academic discussion. Presentation needs some clarification. Study/training texts such as straightforward presentations and discussions adequately organised. Fairly frequent lapses in style and fluency but these do not interfere with basic communication. Controls a moderate range of academic language and specialist terminology in own field. Fairly frequent errors in usage and obvious L1 speech features impair communication at times.
4	Handles simple study/training speech situations with good confidence and competence, but some limitations on moderate-level situations. Conveys short, simple study/training message but with loss of detail and interest. Frequent need to repeat and rephrase. Restricted participation in freer academic discussions. Study/training text organisation is haphazard and requires frequent repair. Little variation in academic style or sense of appropriacy. Frequent false starts and hesitations. Controls a limited range of academic language and specialist terminology in own field. Heavy L1 accent and frequent errors of usage impede intelligibility.
3	Handles simple study/training speech situations with adequate confidence and competence, but many problems with moderate-level situations. Conveys the basic study/training message but with little detail or clarity. Communication breaks down as language constraints interfere with message. Makes basic contributions to academic discussions. Little organisation in study/training texts. Little appreciation of academic style. Restricted to handling basic facts. False starts and hesitations impair communication in study/training contexts. Has a narrow range of academic language and the most common specialist terms in own field. Shortcomings in basic usage and pronunciation cause very frequent problems with training.
2	Handles simple study/training speech situations with erratic confidence and competence. Conveys the shortest, simplest and most factual aspects of the study/training message, such as basic instructions and factual information. At the margins of communication. Constant need for repair. Study/training text organisation is restricted to responding to predictable instructions or expressing basic needs. Sympathetic supervisor is needed to maintain communication. No appreciation of academic style. Has a very narrow range of academic language and a few specialist terms. Shortcomings of basic usage and pronunciation make training in the spoken mode very limited.
1	Handles only the simplest study/training speech situations, eg isolated instructions. Handles these with uncertain confidence and little competence. Any study/training message is difficult to comprehend. Produces study/training texts restricted to groups of words or responses to predictable instructions. Has a basic range of specialist language such as terms similar to those in own L1. L1 speech features and limited language make training in the spoken mode very difficult to conduct or comprehend.

YARDSTICK 14
Stage IV: Reading for social and personal purposes

Typical tasks: Reading private and personal business correspondence, public advertisements, notices and documents, newspapers and magazines, books of fiction and non-fiction, reference sources such as catalogues, dictionaries, etc.

9	Reads all social/personal texts in areas of own and related interests with confidence and competence similar to those in own mother tongue. An exceptional level of social/personal reading. Extracts the complete message from social/personal texts without undue need for dictionary or re-reading. Skilfully processes and evaluates the content and intent for application or relaying. Easily handles extended and complex texts from social/personal sources read at high speed. Reading strategies comparable with those in mother tongue. Handles a complete range of social language in own and a broad range of related interests. Compensates easily for misprints and errors in texts of a social/personal nature.
8	Reads a full range of social/personal texts with confidence and competence which approach those in own mother tongue. Extracts the full message from social/personal texts with only occasional loss of detail or subtlety or need for repair. Uses a full range of techniques to evaluate, apply or relay the content and intent. Flexibly adjusts reading speeds and strategies to long and detailed social/personal texts written in a full range of styles. Handles a full range of social language in own and all related areas of interest. Compensates fully for misprints and errors in texts of a social/personal nature.
7	Reads a wide range of social/personal texts with good confidence and competence. Extracts the majority of the message from social/personal texts with only minor loss of detail or subtlety, and with little need for repair. Uses a wide range of techniques to evaluate, apply or relay the content and intent of the message. Strategies widely effective for reading social/personal texts at normal speed, but less flexible than in own mother tongue. Handles a wide range of social language in own and related areas of interest. Little difficulty in compensating for misprints or errors in texts of a social/personal nature.
6	Reads moderate-level social/personal texts with good confidence and competence, but some difficulties with higher-level texts, especially if opportunities to re-read or refer to a dictionary are restricted. Extracts most of the message from social/personal texts, but with noticeable loss of subtlety and detail. Some need for repair. Uses a good range of techniques to apply or relay the content and intent. Uses flexible strategies and good reading speed for social/personal texts, but with some problems of initial adjustment to style or organisation. Handles a good range of social language in areas of general and own particular interests. Usually manages to compensate for misprints or errors in texts of a social/personal nature.

5	Reads moderate-level social/personal texts with adequate confidence and competence. Extracts the major points of the message from social/personal texts but with frequent loss of detail and subtlety, and frequent need for repair. Uses a fair range of techniques to apply or relay the message. Reads straightforward social/personal texts in areas of own interests and needs at normal speed. Handles a moderate range of social language in areas of general and own particular interests. Sometimes manages to compensate for misprints or errors in texts of a social/personal nature.
4	Reads simple social/personal texts with good confidence and competence, but some limitations on moderate-level texts, especially if opportunities to re-read or refer to a dictionary are restricted. Extracts the broad outline of the message from social/personal texts but with great loss of detail and little concept of subtlety. Uses a limited range of techniques to apply or relay the content and intent. Limited ability to read social/personal texts in areas of own interests or needs. Reading speed and flexibility restricted by frequent need to re-read or refer to a dictionary. Handles a limited range of social language relating to own particular needs or interests. Occasionally manages to compensate for misprints or errors in texts of a social/personal nature.
3	Reads simple social/personal texts with adequate confidence and competence, but many difficulties with moderate-level texts, especially if opportunities to re-read or refer to a dictionary are restricted. Comprehends the gist of the message of social/personal texts but with little detail; alternatively, extracts needed or predicted items of isolated information. Takes patchy notes (probably in L1). Greatly limited ability to read social/personal texts; reads slowly. Requires constant opportunities to re-read or refer to a dictionary. Handles a narrow range of social language relating to own particular needs or interests. Unlikely to compensate for misprints or errors in texts of a social/personal nature.
2	Reads simple social/personal texts with erratic confidence and competence. Comprehends isolated points of the message of social/personal texts and can identify the topic under discussion. Further comprehension depends on L1 or visual support. Takes note of basic factual or numerical information, eg prices, times, dates, sizes, temperatures, etc. Mostly reads very brief social/personal texts. Reads very slowly, constantly re-reading or referring to a dictionary. Handles a very narrow range of social language in areas of immediate needs or interests. Unable to compensate for misprints or errors in texts of a social/personal nature.
1	Reads the simplest and briefest social/personal texts such as public notices, signs, telephone directories, etc. Reads with uncertain confidence and competence. Identifies the topic or basic message of a social/personal text. Further comprehension requires translation or accompanying visuals. Ability to apply or relay message limited by level of comprehension. Reads the briefest social/personal texts such as traffic signs or door notices below sentence level. Reads extremely slowly. Handles a basic range of social language such as international terms similar to those in L1 (eg taxi, telephone, etc.). Unlikely to recognise misprints or errors in texts of a social/personal nature.

YARDSTICK 15

Stage IV: Reading for business purposes

Typical tasks: Reading internal and external business correspondence, publicity and marketing documents, reports and manuals, business journals and press releases, reference sources such as handbooks, catalogues, etc., abbreviated documents such as cables and telexes, standard pro-formas, records, etc.

9	Reads all business texts in areas of own and related areas of responsibility with confidence and competence similar to those in mother tongue. An exceptional level of business reading. Extracts the complete message from a business document without undue need for re-reading or a dictionary. Uses a comprehensive range of techniques to store or relay the message for later business application. Easily handles extended and complex business texts read at high speed. Reading strategies comparable with those in own mother tongue. Handles a complete range of business language and specialist terminology in own and a broad range of related fields. Compensates easily for misprints and errors in business texts.
8	Reads a full range of business texts with confidence and competence which approach those in own mother tongue. Extracts the full message from business texts with only occasional loss of detail and subtlety, or need for repair. Uses a full range of techniques to store or relay the message for business application. Flexibly adjusts reading speeds and strategies to long and detailed business texts written in a full range of styles. Handles a full range of business language and specialist terminology in own and all related fields. Compensates fully for misprints and errors in business texts.
7	Reads a wide range of business texts with good confidence and competence. Extracts the majority of the message from business documents with only minor loss of detail or subtlety, and with little need for repair. Uses a wide range of techniques to store or relay the message for later business application. Strategies widely effective for reading business texts at normal speed, but less flexible than in own mother tongue. Handles a wide range of business language and specialist terminology in own and related fields. Little difficulty in compensating for misprints and errors in business texts.
6	Reads moderate-level business texts with good confidence and competence, but some difficulties with higher-level texts, especially when opportunities to re-read or refer to a dictionary are limited. Extracts most of the message from business documents but with noticeable loss of detail and subtlety. Some need for repair. Uses a good range of techniques to store or relay the message for application. Uses flexible strategies and good reading speed for business texts, but some problems of initial adjustment to style or organisation. Handles a good range of business language and specialist terminology in own field. Usually manages to compensate for misprints and errors in business texts.

5	Reads moderate-level business texts with adequate confidence and competence. Extracts the major points of the message from business documents but with frequent loss of detail and subtlety, and frequent need for repair. Uses a fair range of techniques to store or relay the message for later business application. Reads straightforward business texts in own field at normal speed. Handles a moderate range of business language and specialist terminology in own field. Sometimes manages to compensate for misprints and errors in business texts.
4	Reads simple business texts with good confidence and competence, but some limitations on moderate-level texts, especially when opportunities to re-read or refer to a dictionary are restricted. Extracts the broad outline of the message from business documents, but with great loss of detail and subtlety. Uses a limited range of techniques to store or relay the message for later business application. Limited ability to read business texts in own field. Reading speed and flexibility restricted by frequent need to re-read or refer to a dictionary. Handles a limited range of business language and specialist terminology relating directly to own field. Occasionally manages to compensate for misprints and errors in business texts.
3	Reads simple business texts with adequate confidence and competence, but many difficulties with moderate-level texts, especially when opportunities to re-read or refer to a dictionary are restricted. Comprehends the gist of the message of business documents but with little detail; alternatively, extracts needed or predicted items. Takes brief notes (probably in L1) but with missing information. Greatly limited ability to handle business texts; reads slowly. Requires constant opportunities to re-read or refer to a dictionary. Handles a narrow range of business language and the most common specialist terms in own field. Unlikely to compensate for misprints or errors in business texts.
2	Reads simple and routine business texts with erratic confidence and competence. Comprehends isolated points of the message of business texts and can identify the topic under discussion. Further comprehension depends on L1 or visual support. Takes notes of basic factual or numerical information, eg prices, quantities, delivery dates, destinations, times of despatch or arrival, etc. Mostly reads very brief business texts and routine forms. Reads very slowly, constantly re-reading and referring to a dictionary. Handles a very narrow range of business language and a few specialist terms. Unable to compensate for misprints or errors in business texts.
1	Reads the simplest, briefest and most routine business texts such as addresses, warning signs or headings and data on standard forms. Reads with uncertain confidence and competence. Identifies the topic or basic message of a business document and extracts isolated information from standard forms. Further comprehension requires translation or accompanying visuals. Ability to apply or relay message limited by level of comprehension. Reads the most basic business texts, usually below sentence level. Reads extremely slowly. Handles a basic range of business language such as terms similar to those in L1. Unlikely to recognise misprints or errors in business texts.

YARDSTICK 16

Stage 1V: Reading for study/training purposes

Typical tasks: Reading academic textbooks, papers and journals, workshop and instruction manuals, institutional regulations and guidance, etc.

9	Reads all study/training texts in own and related fields with confidence and competence similar to those in own mother tongue. An exceptional level of study reading. Extracts the complete message from study/training texts without undue need for repair. Uses a comprehensive range of note-taking and retrieval techniques for later study applications. Easily handles extended and complex study/training texts read at high speed. Academic reading strategies comparable with those in own mother tongue. Handles a complete range of academic language and specialist terminology in own and a broad range of related fields. Compensates easily for misprints and errors in study/training texts.
8	Reads a full range of study/training texts with confidence and competence which approach those in own mother tongue. Extracts the full message from study/training texts with only occasional loss of detail or subtlety. Uses a full range of note-taking and retrieval techniques for later study applications. Flexibly adjusts reading speeds and strategies to long and detailed study/training texts written in a full range of styles. Handles a full range of academic language and specialist terminology in own and related specialist fields. Fully compensates for misprints and errors in study/training texts.
7	Reads a wide range of study/training texts with good confidence and competence. Extracts the majority of the message from study/training texts with only minor loss of detail and subtlety, and with little need for repair. Uses a wide range of note-taking and retrieval techniques. Strategies widely effective for reading study/training texts read at normal speed, but less flexible than those in own mother tongue. Handles a wide range of academic language and specialist terminology in own and related fields. Little difficulty in compensating for misprints or errors in study/training texts.
6	Reads moderate-level study/training texts with good confidence and competence, but some difficulties with higher-level texts, especially if opportunities to re-read or refer to a dictionary are limited. Extracts most of the message from study/training texts but with noticeable loss of detail and subtlety. Some need for repair. Uses a good range of note-taking and retrieval techniques for later application. Uses flexible strategies and good reading speed for study/training texts, but some problems with initial adjustment to style or organisation. Handles a good range of academic language and specialist terminology in own field. Usually manages to compensate for misprints and errors in study/training texts.

5	Reads moderate-level study/training texts with adequate confidence and competence. Extracts the major points of the message from study/training texts but with frequent loss of detail and subtlety, and frequent need for repair. Uses a fair range of note-taking and retrieval techniques for later study application. Reads straightforward study/training texts in own field at normal speed. Handles a moderate range of academic language and specialist terminology in own field. Occasionally manages to compensate for misprints or errors in study/training texts.
4	Reads simple study/training texts with good confidence and competence, but some limitations on moderate-level texts, especially when opportunities to re-read or refer to a dictionary are restricted. Extracts the broad outline of the message from study/training texts, but with great loss of detail and subtlety. Uses a limited range of note-taking techniques for later study applications. Limited ability to read study/training texts in own field. Reading speed and flexibility limited by frequent need to re-read and refer to a dictionary. Handles a limited range of academic language and specialist terminology relating directly to own field. Occasionally manages to compensate for misprints or errors in study/training texts.
3	Reads simple study/training texts with adequate confidence and competence, but many difficulties with moderate-level texts, especially when opportunities to re-read or refer to a dictionary are restricted. Comprehends the gist of the message of study/training texts but with little detail; alternatively, extracts needed or predicted items. Takes brief notes (probably in L1) but with missing information. Greatly limited ability to handle study/training texts; reads slowly. Requires constant opportunities to re-read or refer to a dictionary. Handles a narrow range of academic language and the most common specialist terms in own field. Unlikely to manage to compensate for misprints or errors in study/training texts.
2	Reads simple study/training texts with erratic confidence and competence. Comprehends isolated points of the message of study/training texts and can identify the topic under discussion. Further comprehension depends on L1 abstract, visual aids or an accompanying demonstration. Takes brief notes on basic factual or numerical information, eg formulae, dates, references, etc. Mostly reads very brief study/training texts. Reads very slowly, constantly re-reading and referring to a dictionary. Handles a very narrow range of academic language and a few specialist terms. Unable to compensate for misprints and errors in study/training texts.
1	Reads the simplest and briefest study/training texts, such as isolated instructions. Handles them with little confidence and uncertain competence, especially if opportunities for repair are limited. Identifies the topic or basic message of training texts or instructions. Further comprehension requires translation, accompanying visuals or demonstrations. Note-taking restricted by level of comprehension. Handles the briefest training texts, such as isolated instructions below sentence level. Reads extremely slowly. Handles a basic range of specialist language such as terms similar to those in L1. Unlikely to recognise misprints or errors in study/training texts.

YARDSTICK 17

Stage IV: Writing for social and personal purposes

Typical tasks: Writing private and personal correspondence; articles and stories; completing standard forms and documents (eg when travelling); writing abbreviated messages such as notes and cables, etc.

9	Writes all social/personal texts in areas of own and related interests with confidence and competence similar to those in own mother tongue. An exceptional level of social/personal writing. Social/personal message is completely conveyed with total relevance and high interest. Writing is completely adjusted to reader's interests and knowledge of the language. Social/personal texts such as extended and complex letters or articles are well organised and sustained. Writes at high speed. Style and layout completely appropriate to context and purpose. Controls a complete range of social language in own and a broad range of related interests. Complete accuracy of usage and spelling apart from occasional 'slips'.
8	Writes a full range of social/personal texts with confidence and competence which approach those in own mother tongue. Social/personal message is fully conveyed with interesting and attractive treatment. Writing is fully adjusted to reader's interests and knowledge of the language. Social/personal texts such as long and detailed letters or articles are well organised and sustained. Writes at speed. Style fully appropriate to context and purpose. Controls a full range of social language in own and related areas of interest. Only minor errors and 'slips' of usage and spelling.
7	Writes a wide range of social/personal texts with confidence and competence. Social/personal message is clearly conveyed and with interest. Writing is well adjusted to reader's interests and knowledge of the language. Social/personal texts such as letters or articles are clearly organised. Occasional lack of fluency or flexibility. Occasional uncertainties over appropriate style. Controls a wide range of social language in own and related areas of interest. Occasional errors of usage and spelling, but these do not reduce communicative effect.
6	Writes moderate-level social/personal texts with good confidence and competence, but some difficulties with higher-level texts. Basic ideas of social/personal message are adequately conveyed but with noticeable loss of subtlety. Writing is adequately adjusted to reader's interests and knowledge of the language. Social/personal texts such as letters or articles are adequately organised but with some lapses in cohesion. Some sense of appropriate style. Writing often lacks fluency. Controls a good range of social language in areas of general and own particular interests. Noticeable errors of usage and spelling but these do not reduce communicative effect.

5	Writes moderate-level social/personal texts with adequate confidence and competence. Social/personal message is broadly conveyed but with little subtlety and some loss of detail. Thread of message may not always be clear and reader may have to backtrack to clarify. Social/personal texts such as straightforward letters or short articles are adequately organised. Fairly frequent lapses in style and fluency but these do not interfere with communication of basic ideas. Controls a moderate range of social language in areas of general and own particular needs. Fairly frequent errors in usage and spelling impair communication at times.
4	Writes simple social/personal texts with good confidence and competence, but some limitations on moderate-level texts. Conveys short social/personal messages but with loss of detail and subtlety. Lack of clarity requires reader to backtrack frequently. Marginally communicative as a social/personal writer. Social/personal text organisation is haphazard. Little variation in style or sense of appropriacy to context or purpose. Frequent lapses of fluency when writing. Controls a limited range of social language relating to own particular needs and interests. Frequent errors of usage and spelling impede clarity of message.
3	Writes simple social/personal texts with adequate confidence and competence, but many problems with moderate-level texts. Conveys basic social/personal message but with little detail or clarity. Communication breaks down as language limitations interfere with message. Little sense of reader's expectations. Little organisation of social/personal texts. Little appreciation of style. Restricted to handling basic facts in short paragraphs. Basic punctuation. Has a narrow range of social language in areas relating to own particular needs or interests. Regular inaccuracies in basic usage and spelling cause very frequent problems.
2	Writes simple social/personal texts with erratic confidence and competence. Conveys the shortest, simplest and most factual aspects of the social/personal message. Little or no detail or amplification. Writes very slowly, constantly re-writing and referring to a dictionary. Social/personal text organisation is restricted to sentence-level responses to headings or questions in questionnaires or forms. No appreciation of style. Erratic punctuation. Has a very narrow range of social language relating to own particular needs or interests. Many inaccuracies in basic usage make social/personal communication in the written mode very limited.
1	Writes the simplest social/personal texts, eg completing forms or documents with personal or travel details, or factual or numerical data, mostly at the word level. Handles these with uncertain confidence and little competence. Any social/personal message is very difficult to construct or comprehend. Produces social/personal texts restricted to words or groups of words in response to predictable headings or questions. Has a basic range of social language such as international terms similar to those in L1 (eg hotel, airport, etc.). Linguistic restrictions, spelling and handwriting make any writing difficult to comprehend.

YARDSTICK 18
Stage IV: Writing for business purposes

Typical tasks: Writing internal and external business correspondence, publicity and marketing documents, reports and manuals, business articles and press releases, abbreviated documents such as cables and telexes, standard pro-formas and records, etc.

9	Writes all business texts in own and related areas of responsibility with confidence and competence which approach those in own mother tongue. An exceptional level of business writing. Business message is completely conveyed with total relevance and high interest. Writing is completely adjusted to readers' knowledge of topic and language. Full use of supporting visual devices. Business texts such as extended and complex reports are coherently organised. Writes at high speed. Style and display conventions completely appropriate for context and purpose. Controls a complete range of business language and specialist terminology in own and a broad range of fields. Complete accuracy of usage and spelling apart from occasional 'slips'.
8	Writes a full range of business texts with confidence and competence which approach those in own mother tongue. Business message is fully conveyed with interesting and attractive treatment. Writing is fully adjusted to readers' knowledge of topic and language. Full use of supporting visual devices. Business texts such as long and detailed reports and manuals are well organised and sustained. Writes at speed. Style and display conventions fully appropriate to context and purpose. Controls a full range of business language and specialist terminology in own and related fields. Only minor errors and 'slips' of usage and spelling.
7	Writes a wide range of business texts with good confidence and competence. Business message is clearly conveyed and with interest. Writing is well adjusted to readers' knowledge of topic and language. Uses a wide range of supporting visual devices. Business texts such as reports, letters or manuals are clearly organised. Occasional lack of fluency or flexibility. Occasional uncertainties over appropriate style or business display conventions. Controls a wide range of business language and specialist terminology in own and related fields. Occasional errors of usage and spelling, but these do not reduce communicative effect.
6	Writes moderate-level business texts with good confidence and competence, but some difficulties with higher-level texts. Basic ideas of business message are adequately conveyed but with noticeable loss of subtlety. Writing is adequately adjusted to readers' knowledge of topic and language. Good use of supporting visuals. Business texts such as reports, letters or manuals are adequately organised but with some lapses in cohesion. Some sense of appropriate style. Writing often lacks fluency. Controls a good range of business language and specialist terminology in own field. Noticeable errors of usage and spelling but these do not reduce communicative effect.

5	Writes moderate-level business texts with adequate confidence and competence. Business message is broadly conveyed but with little subtlety and some loss of detail. Thread of message may not always be clear and reader may have to backtrack to clarify. Some use of visuals. Business texts such as straightforward letters and short reports are adequately organised. Fairly frequent lapses in style and fluency but these do not interfere with communication of basic ideas. Controls a moderate range of business language and specialist terminology in own field. Fairly frequent errors in usage and spelling impair communication at times.
4	Writes simple business texts with good confidence and competence, but some limitations on moderate-level texts. Conveys short business messages but with loss of detail and subtlety. Lack of clarity requires reader to backtrack frequently. Marginally communicative as a business writer. Business text organisation is haphazard. Little variation in business style or sense of appropriacy to context or audience. Frequent lapses of fluency when writing. Controls a limited range of business language and specialist terminology in own field. Frequent errors in usage and spelling impede clarity of message.
3	Writes simple business texts with adequate confidence and competence, but many problems with moderate-level texts. Conveys the basic business message but with little detail or clarity. Communication breaks down as language limitations interfere with message. Little sense of readers' expectations. Little organisation of business texts. Little appreciation of business style or display conventions. Restricted to handling basic facts in short paragraphs. Basic punctuation. Has a narrow range of business language and the most common specialist terms in own fields. Regular inaccuracies in basic usage and spelling cause very frequent problems with business in the written mode.
2	Writes simple business texts with erratic confidence and competence. Conveys the shortest, simplest and most factual aspects of the business message. Little or no detail or amplification. Writes very slowly, constantly rewriting and referring to a dictionary. Business text organisation is restricted to sentence-level responses to headings or questions in pro-formas etc. No appreciation of business style. Erratic punctuation and display. Has a very narrow range of business language with a few specialist terms. Many inaccuracies in basic usage and spelling make business in the written mode very limited.
1	Writes the simplest business texts, eg completing forms and pro-formas with personal or company details, or factual or numerical data, mostly at the word level. Handles these with uncertain confidence and little competence. Any business message is very difficult to construct or comprehend. Produces business texts restricted to words or groups of words in response to predictable headings or questions. Has a basic range of specialist language such as terms similar to those in L1. Linguistic restrictions, spelling and handwriting make business texts very difficult to construct or comprehend.

YARDSTICK 19
Stage IV: Writing for study/training purposes

Typical tasks: Writing academic essays, papers, articles, etc, writing workshop and instruction manuals; completing instruction sheets, workshop or laboratory worksheets, etc.

9	Writes all study/training texts in own and related specialist fields with confidence and competence which approach those in own mother tongue. An exceptional level of study/training writing. Study/training message is completely conveyed with total relevance and high interest. Writing is completely adjusted to students'/trainees' knowledge of topic and language. Full use of visuals. Study/training texts such as extended and complex papers or manuals are coherently organised. Writes at high speed. Style and academic conventions completely appropriate to context and purpose. Controls a complete range of academic language and specialist terminology in own and a broad range of fields. Complete accuracy of usage apart from occasional 'slips'.
8	Writes a full range of study/training texts with confidence and competence which approach those in own mother tongue. Study/training message is fully conveyed with interesting and attractive treatment. Writing is fully adjusted to students'/trainees' knowledge of topic and language. Full use of visual devices. Study/training texts such as long and detailed papers and manuals are well organised and sustained. Writes at speed. Style and academic conventions fully appropriate to context and purpose. Controls a full range of academic language and specialist terminology in own and related fields.
7	Writes a wide range of study/training texts with good confidence and competence. Study/training message is clearly conveyed and with interest. Writing is well adjusted to students'/trainees' knowledge of topic and language. Uses a wide range of supporting visual devices. Study/training texts such as papers or manuals are clearly organised. Occasional lack of fluency and flexibility. Occasional uncertainties over appropriate style or academic conventions. Controls a wide range of academic language and specialist terminology in own and related fields. Occasional errors of usage and spelling, but these do not reduce communicative effect.
6	Writes moderate-level study/training texts with good confidence and competence, but some difficulties with higher-level texts. Basic ideas of study/training message are adequately conveyed but with noticeable loss of subtlety. Writing is adequately adjusted to students'/trainees' knowledge of topic and language. Study/training texts such as papers and manuals are adequately organised but with some lapses in cohesion. Some sense of academic style appropriate to context and purpose. Writing often lacks fluency. Controls a good range of academic language and specialist terminology in own field. Noticeable errors of usage and spelling but these rarely reduce communicative effect.

5	Writes moderate-level study/training texts with adequate confidence and competence. Study/training message is broadly conveyed but with little subtlety and some loss of detail. Thread of argument may not always be clear and reader may have to backtrack to clarify. Study/training texts such as straightforward papers and manuals adequately organised. Fairly frequent lapses in style and fluency but these do not interfere with communication of basic ideas. Controls a moderate range of academic language and specialist terminology in own field. Fairly frequent errors in usage and spelling impair communication at times.
4	Writes simple study/training texts with good confidence and competence, but some limitations on moderate-level texts. Conveys short study/training message but with loss of detail and subtlety. Lack of clarity requires reader to backtrack frequently. Marginally communicative as an academic writer. Study/training text organisation is haphazard. Little variation in academic style or sense of appropriacy to context or audience. Frequent lapses in fluency when writing. Controls a limited range of academic language and specialist terminology in own field. Frequent errors in usage and spelling impede clarity of message.
3	Writes simple study/training texts with adequate confidence and competence, but many problems with moderate-level texts. Conveys the basic study/training message but with little detail or clarity. Communication breaks down as language constraints interfere with message. Little sense of student/trainee/trainer expectations. Little organisation of study/training texts. Little appreciation of academic style. Restricted to handling basic facts in short paragraphs or worksheet responses. Basic punctuation and layout. Has a narrow range of academic language and the most common specialist terms in own field. Regular inaccuracies in basic usage and spelling cause very frequent problems with training in written mode.
2	Writes simple study/training texts with erratic confidence and competence. Conveys the shortest, simplest and most factual aspects of the study/training message. Little or no detail or amplification. Writes very slowly, constantly rewriting and referring to a dictionary. Study/training text organisation is restricted to sentence-level responses to headings or questions on worksheets, etc. No appreciation of academic style. Erratic punctuation and layout. Has a very narrow range of academic language with a few specialist terms. Many inaccuracies in basic usage make training in the written mode very limited.
1	Writes the simplest study/training texts, eg completing forms or worksheets with personal details, or factual or numerical data, mostly at the word level. Handles these with uncertain confidence and little competence. Any study/training message is very difficult to construct or comprehend. Produces study/training texts restricted to words or groups of words in response to predictable headings, questions or instructions. Has a basic range of specialist language such as terms similar to those in L1. Linguistic restrictions, spelling and handwriting make training texts very difficult to construct or comprehend.

YARDSTICK 20
Stage V: Linguistic skills

	Mastery of grammar, vocabulary, style and textual cohesion
9	Applies a complete range of linguistic skills with confidence and competence similar to those in own mother tongue. An exceptional level of linguistic skill. Message presentation is completely adjusted to audience's knowledge of the language. No undue need for language repair. Text is coherently organised with a complete mastery of cohesive devices. Uses a complete range of styles totally appropriate to context and purpose. Has a complete range of language structures and vocabulary. Applies a complete command of linguistic accuracy to communication and examination tasks.
8	Applies a full range of linguistic skills with confidence and competence which approach those in own mother tongue. Presentation of message is fully adjusted to audience's knowledge of the language. Only occasional need for language repair. Text is organised with full coherence and a full range of cohesive devices. Uses a full range of styles appropriate to context and purpose. Has a full range of language structures and vocabulary. Applies a full command of linguistic accuracy to communication and examination tasks.
7	Applies a wide range of linguistic skills with good confidence and competence. Presentation of message is well adjusted to audience's knowledge of the language. Little need for repair. Text is well organised with a wide range of cohesive devices. Uses a good range of styles appropriate to context and purpose. Has a wide range of language structures and vocabulary. Applies a very good grasp of accuracy to communication and examination tasks.
6	Applies linguistic skills to moderate-level tasks with good confidence and competence, but some problems with higher-level tasks. Presentation of message is adequately adjusted to audience's knowledge of the language. Some need for language repair. Text is adequately organised with a good range of cohesive devices. Uses a fair range of styles and some uncertainties over appropriacy. Has a good range of language structures and vocabulary. Applies a good grasp of accuracy to communication and examination tasks.
5	Applies linguistic skills to moderate-level tasks with adequate confidence and competence. Presentation of basic message is adequately adjusted to audience's knowledge of the language. Fairly frequent language lapses necessitate repair to capture detail and subtlety. Basic organisation of text is adequate, with a moderate range of cohesive devices. Uses a moderate range of styles but lapses of appropriacy are fairly frequent. Has a moderate range of language structures and vocabulary. Applies a moderate grasp of accuracy to communication and examination tasks.

4	Applies linguistic skills to simple tasks with good confidence and competence, but some limitations on moderate-level tasks. Message is exchanged using a limited language repertoire. Lacks the resources to adjust presentation to audience's knowledge of the language. Frequent need for repair to clarify detail. Text organisation is haphazard with a limited range of cohesive devices. Little capacity for stylistic variation or appropriacy. Has a limited range of language structures and vocabulary. Applies a limited grasp of accuracy to communication and examination tasks.
3	Applies linguistic skills to simple tasks with adequate confidence and competence, but many problems with moderate-level tasks. Language limitations interfere with the message; constant need for language repair in order to exchange message. Has little appreciation of text organisation and a narrow range of cohesive devices. Little appreciation of stylistic variation or appropriacy. Has a narrow range of language structures and vocabulary. Applies a basic level of linguistic accuracy to communication and examination tasks.
2	Applies linguistic skills to simple tasks with erratic confidence and competence. Message is exchanged through constant negotiation and repair of the language. Text organisation is restricted to sequencing and the most basic cohesive devices. No appreciation of stylistic variation or appropriacy. Has a very narrow range of language structure and vocabulary. Has little grasp of accuracy to apply to communication or examination tasks.
1	Applies linguistic skills to the simplest tasks with uncertain confidence and little competence. Message is difficult to exchange because of language limitations. Constant and repeated negotiation and repair essential. Text organisation is limited to the structure of the interaction or the layout of the input text. No use of cohesive devices apart from simple co-ordination. No grasp of style or appropriacy. Has a basic range of language structure and vocabulary. Has no grasp of linguistic accuracy to apply to communication or examination tasks.

YARDSTICK 21
Stage V: Functional skills

Size of functional repertoire; range and subtlety of realisations; sequencing of functions to create text coherence; selection of functions appropriate to style, context and purpose; application of functions to carry out tasks through language - eg conveying ideas, influencing others, establishing interpersonal relationships, extending knowledge, imaginative expression, etc.

9	Applies a complete range of functional skills with confidence and competence similar to those in own mother tongue. An exceptional level of functional skill. Extracts and conveys message by selecting functions and realisations completely adjusted to purpose. No undue need for repair to clarify the speaker's/writer's communicative intention. Sequences functions to produce a completely coherent text. Functional realisations are completely appropriate to context and purpose. Selects from a complete range of language functions and realisations. Applies these with complete accuracy.
8	Applies a full range of functional skills with confidence and competence which approach those in own mother tongue. Extracts and conveys message by selecting functions and realisations fully adjusted to purpose. Occasional need for repair to clarify the speaker's/writer's communicative intention. Sequences functions to produce a fully coherent text. Functional realisations are fully appropriate to context and purpose. Selects from a full range of language functions and realisations. Applies these with full accuracy.
7	Applies a wide range of functional skills with good confidence and competence. Extracts and conveys the message by selecting functions and realisations well adjusted to purpose. Little need for repair to clarify speaker's/writer's communicative intention. Sequences functions to produce a text with very good coherence. Functional realisations are appropriate to context and purpose. Selects from a wide range of language functions and realisations. Applies these with very good accuracy.
6	Applies functional skills with good confidence and competence, but some problems with higher-level tasks. Extracts and conveys message by selecting functions and realisations adequately adjusted to purpose. Some need for repair to clarify speaker's/writer's communicative intention. Sequences functions to produce a text with adequate coherence. Some uncertainty when selecting realisations which are appropriate to context and purpose. Selects from a good range of language functions and realisations. Applies these with good accuracy.
5	Applies functional skills to moderate-level tasks with adequate confidence and competence. Extracts and conveys the message by selecting functions basically adjusted to purpose. Fairly frequent need for repair to clarify speaker's/writer's communicative intention. Sequences functions to produce a text with basic coherence. Fairly frequent uncertainties and lapses when selecting realisations which are appropriate to context and purpose. Selects from a moderate range of language functions and realisations. Applies these with moderate grasp of accuracy.

4	Applies functional skills to simple tasks with good confidence and competence, but some limitations on moderate-level tasks. Extracts and conveys the message by selecting from a limited range of functions and realisations. Frequent need for repair to clarify or establish speaker's/writer's communicative intention. Sequences functions to produce a text with inconsistent coherence. Frequent lapses when selecting realisations which are appropriate to context and purpose. Has a limited range of language functions and realisations. Applies these with a limited grasp of accuracy.
3	Applies functional skills to simple tasks with adequate confidence and competence but many problems with moderate-level tasks. Limitations of functional range restrict message to extracting and conveying simple practical needs. Constant need for repair to clarify or establish speaker's/writer's communicative intention. Arranges functions to produce a text with linear sequence, eg simple narrative or question-answer. Lacks the functional range to select realisations appropriate to context. Has a narrow range of language functions and few realisations for each function. Applies these with a basic grasp of accuracy.
2	Applies functional skills to simple tasks with erratic confidence and competence. Functional range restricts message to extracting and conveying basic needs. Constant negotiation and repair needed to clarify or establish speaker's/writer's communicative intention. Arranges functions to produce a text with simple sequence. Has no appreciation of functional appropriacy when selecting realisations. Has a very narrow range of language functions and unlikely to have more than a single realisation of each function. Applies these with little grasp of accuracy.
1	Applies functional skills to the simplest tasks with uncertain confidence and little competence. Message is difficult to exchange because of functional limitations. Constant and repeated repair is needed to establish speaker's/writer's communicative intention. Text has no coherence beyond that established by the functional sequencing of the interaction (eg greet-response, question-answer). Functional realisations have little appropriacy to context or purpose. Has a basic range of language functions and a single realisation for each function. Applies these with no grasp of accuracy.

YARDSTICK 22
Stage V: Examination skills

9	Applies examination skills to enhance performance on 'difficult' or high-level tasks.	A difficult or high-level task displays some or all of these features: • format – unfamiliar or unpredictable • tasks and rubrics many and/or long items (proportional to time) • constraints – few or no opportunities for repair • stimulus and response requirement – to extract or convey the communicative intent of an extended and complex message • to produce or react to a long and detailed text with a full range of stylistic variations • to produce or comprehend a wide range of language handled with a high degree of accuracy.
8	Applies examination skills to achieve criterion-level performance on 'difficult' tasks.	
7	Applies examination skills at below expected level on 'difficult' tasks.	
6	Applies examination skills to enhance performance on 'moderate' tasks.	A moderate task displays some or all of these features: • format – unfamiliar but predictable or easily comprehended • tasks and rubrics – items of intermediate number and/or length (proportional to time) • constraints – some opportunities for repair • stimulus and response – requirement to extract or convey the communicative intent of a straightforward message • to produce or react to a straightforward text with a moderate range of stylistic variations • to produce or comprehend a moderate range of language handled with a fair degree of accuracy.
5	Applies examination skills to achieve criterion-level performance on 'moderate' tasks.	
4	Applies examination skills at below expected level on 'moderate' tasks.	
3	Applies examination skills to enhance performance on 'simple' tasks.	A simple task displays some or all of these features: • format – familiar and predictable • tasks and rubrics – few and/or short items (proportional to time) • constraints – ample opportunities for repair • stimulus and response – requirement to extract or convey the communicative intent of a simple or basic message; alternatively, no requirement to extract or convey a message • to produce or react to a simple text with a narrow range of stylistic variations • to produce or comprehend a narrow range of language handled with a good degree of accuracy, or a broader range with a lesser degree of accuracy.
2	Applies examination skills to achieve criterion-level performance on 'simple' tasks.	
1	Applies examination skills at below expected level on 'simple' tasks.	

Chapter 6
The Examinations Described

We now give a description of the Framework examinations to supplement the information shown in the Chart. Because very detailed descriptions are given in the *Longman Guide to English Language Examinations*, we will give here an outline of the main features and also comment on those aspects which bear on the structure of Framework. We do advise you to supplement this information by studying the *Longman Guide*. It should be understood that these descriptions are not the official regulations for the examinations - these can be found in the official syllabuses for each Board. We will deal with each examination under the following headings:

Purpose:	the main aims of the examination.
Elements:	an outline of the main components.
Content:	the test topics, tasks and formats with selected examples.
Results:	how presented and their equivalences in ESU Levels.*
Special Features:	notable features of the examination.
Revisions:	changes or new developments in hand (if any).
Availability:	when, where and how to be tested.
Yardsticks:	references to relevant Yardsticks in Chapter 5.

***Note** The estimated minimum level for a Pass is shown either as at a basic ESU level (eg 5) or at the middle of a level (eg 5+).

The examinations are described below in the following order, which closely follows the order of presentation in the Chart. We use here the abbreviated titles of the Boards for ease of reference - the full titles are shown in the relevant sections.

1 ARELS Examinations Trust.

2 Oxford Delegacy.

3 Cambridge Syndicate/Royal Society of Arts.

4 City and Guilds.

5 English-Speaking Board.

6 Institute of Linguists.

7 London University.

8 Trinity College London.

9 National Board of Speech and Drama.

10 Pitman Examinations Institute.

11 London Chamber of Commerce.

12 Associated Examining Board.

13 English Language Testing Service.

14 Joint Matriculation Board.

15 North West Regional Examinations Board.

The addresses of these Boards will be found in Appendix B on pages 104-106.

6.1 ARELS

The Association of Recognised English Language Schools Examinations Trust

Oral Examinations

Purpose To provide assessments of proficiency in using and understanding spoken English.

Elements

Level	*Listen*	*Speak*	*Time*
Preliminary/Junior	•	•	30 mins
Higher	•	•	50 mins
Diploma	•	•	50 mins

Content Topics are taken from everyday, realistic situations. The tasks given test English as a means of communication rather than as an academic exercise. The main test formats at the appropriate levels are:

Writing numbers, letters and abbreviations. Giving brief answers to factual questions. Giving suitable responses to questions. Marking a map or plan or listening to a conversation. Choosing the most suitable of a set of pictures.

Selecting one of several options to show understanding of a spoken passage.

Extended speaking in an appropriate situation, for up to one minute. To include explanations, advice, requests. Free speaking for up to two minutes on a prepared topic chosen from a list.

Results The Preliminary examination has three grades of Pass and two of failure. The Higher and Diploma examinations have seven grades of pass and two of failure. The ESU Level equivalents are estimated to be:

ARELS		**ESU Level**
Preliminary	Pass	3+
	Good Pass	4+
	Very Good Pass	5
Higher	Pass	6
	Credit	6+
	Distinction	7
Diploma	Pass	8

Special Features The ARELS Examinations concentrate on the listening and speaking skills; the complementary reading and writing skills are examined by the Oxford Delegacy examinations described in the next section. The ARELS Examinations are on master tapes and candidates' responses are recorded for central marking.

Availability The ARELS Examinations are available worldwide. Current numbers being examined are approximately 10,000 candidates per year, mainly in Britain, mainland Europe, South America and the Far East. Regular sessions are held in March, May/June and November but opportunity testing is available at any time.

Yardsticks Chapter 5: 1 2 4 5 8 11 21

6.2 Oxford Delegacy

The University of Oxford Delegacy of Local Examinations

English as a Foreign Language

Purpose To test the practical reading and writing skills which a person would need in an English-speaking environment.

Elements

Level	*Read*	*Write*	*Time*
Preliminary/Junior	•	•	4 hr
Higher	•	•	4 hr 30 min

Content The topics are those met in everyday situations. The tasks are as realistic as possible, using authentic printed materials. The main test formats, varied in difficulty at the appropriate levels, are:

Writing both formal and informal letters, messages, telegrams and notices, a composition on given familiar topics and situations with guidance by notes, advertisements, etc. Converting a dialogue or situation into a message. Reading comprehension of texts involving use of dictionary, form-filling, following instructions, and use of drawings or maps. Realistic writing tasks such as reports, summaries, expansions and comparison of information sources.

Results Shown as Pass, Credit or Distinction and two grades of Fail. ESU Level equivalents are estimated as:

Oxford		**ESU Level**
Preliminary	Pass	3+
	Credit	4+
	Distinction	5
Higher	Pass	6
	Credit	6+
	Distinction	7+

Special Features The Oxford Examinations concentrate on reading and writing skills and complement the listening and speaking elements of the ARELS tests already described. The test items make use of authentic source materials - advertisements, maps, articles, etc. - which are particularly attractively produced.

Availability The examination is available both in Britain and worldwide, the annual number of candidates running at about 10,000. Held in March, May/June and November and at other times by arrangement.

Yardsticks Chapter 5: 1 3 6 7 14 17 21

6.3 Cambridge Syndicate
University of Cambridge Local Examinations Syndicate
Royal Society of Arts Examinations Board

(a) Preliminary English Test (PET)

(b) First Certificate in English (FCE)

(c) Certificate of Proficiency in English (CPE)

(d) Diploma of English Studies (DES)

(e) Certificate in English for English Language Teachers (CEELT)

(f) Communicative Use of English as a Foreign Language (CUEFL)

(g) Certificate in English as a Foreign Language for Secretaries (CEFLS)

Purpose The range of exams offered is from elementary to advanced and meets the various language needs of students whether general, academic or for specific purposes eg for Secretaries or Language Teachers.

Elements

Examination	*Read*	*Write*	*Listen*	*Speak*	*Time*
PET	•	•	•	•	2 hr 30 min
FCE	•	•	•	•	5 hr 15 min
CPE	•	•	•	•	1 hr 45 min
DES	•	•			15 hr
CEELT1	•	•	•	•	3 hr 15 min
CEELT 2	•	•	•	•	3 hr 15 min
CUEFL:					
Foundation	•	•	•	•	18 to 28 min
Basic	•	•	•	•	2 hr 45 min
Intermediate	•	•	•	•	3 hr 15 min
Advanced	•	•	•	•	3 hr 45 min
CEFLS	•	•	•	•	2 hr 30 min

Content

Preliminary English Test
The revised Preliminary English Test recognises that language is normally based on an interaction between people, characteristic forms being oral interaction, letter writing,

the completion of forms and the understanding of instructions, notices and advertisements. The Preliminary English Test reflects the desire of most students to acquire English primarily for the purposes of communication. A particular feature of the revised version is the provision of context for the language being tested.

Within a defined context of lexis and structure, candidates will be able to understand public notices and signs, read short texts of a factual nature and show understanding of the content; to demonstrate understanding of the structure of the language as it is used to express notions of relative time, space, possession, etc to scan factual material for information, disregarding redundant or irrelevant material; to read texts of an imaginative or emotional character and appreciate the central sense, the attitude of the writer to his material and the effect it is intended to have on the reader.

First Certificate in English
The First Certificate represents a general standard of competence in English at an intermediate level, and as an effective basis for further study. It has widespread recognition in commerce and industry, eg for public contact or secretarial work, in banking, airlines, catering etc, and in individual university faculties, polytechnics and other institutions.

There are five papers consisting of Reading Comprehension, Composition, Use of English, Listening Comprehension and an Interview.

Certificate of Proficiency in English
The Certificate of Proficiency examination represents an advanced level of competence. It is recognised as fulfilling requirements in English language for matriculation purposes by British universities and many universities in English-speaking countries.

There are five papers, as for the First Certificate in English (see above)

There are also optional additional papers:

1 Translation - candidates are required to translate from, and into, English. Two or more passages of varying style are set.

2 Literature - questions are in the form of passages from a text for comment, and essay questions. Two of each kind must be answered, covering at least three texts.

Diploma of English Studies
DES introduces language and appreciation, tests the ability to express ideas, and show critical appreciation of Literature from a list of set titles.

Candidates must show that they can illustrate general arguments by detailed textual references and relate the authors or texts to the background of the period of study. Questions on British life and institutions are also included which demand breadth and depth of study and the ability to relate the given topic to British history and culture.

Certificate in English for English Language Teachers
The examination, which is offered at two levels, aims to provide an incentive for teachers of English to improve their language proficiency for personal and professional development by focussing on the language teaching classroom and providing tasks related to the work of a language teacher. It is **not** a teaching qualification.

Communicative Use of English as a Foreign Language
The Higher level tasks include:

Reading using a source booklet and answering questions of multiple choice, true/false or short response types. Dictionaries may be used.

Listening from taped source materials, answering questions of multiple choice or gap-filling types.

Writing: produce letters, notes, instructions, guides and reports.

Oral Interaction: an interview with a teacher dealing with personal information, and a given situation; a discussion between candidates in pairs or threes on a given topic.

Certificate in English as a Foreign Language for Secretaries
CEFLS was intended for those students who have already acquired or are acquiring secretarial skills. The aim of the test is to enable a secretary whose first language is not English to function efficiently in an office environment where English is used.

Results

PET expressed as Pass/Fail.

FCE and CPE. Certificates are awarded in Grades A, B, and C.

DES. The Diploma is awarded in First Grade, Upper and Lower Second Grade.

CEELT. Results expressed as a Pass or Fail.

CUEFL. Given as a profile of Pass or Fail at the levels taken. Candidates may take the four skill parts of the examination at any combination of levels in the Basic, Intermediate and Advanced tests.

CEFLS expressed as a Pass/Fail. Candidates must pass on all three papers.

Cambridge	ESU Level
PET	3+
FCE	5
CPE	6+
CEELT 1	6
CEELT 2	7
DES	7+

RSA		ESU Level
CUEFL	Foundation	2
	Basic	4
	Intermediate	5
	Advanced	7
CEFLS		6

Special Features The currency of these exams is established internationally. They offer students a variety of options of level and purpose.

Revisions The structure and content of the CUEFL examinations are under review and Certificates at Upper Intermediate level are being considered.

Availability All the examinations are available worldwide.

PET in March, July/August, October/November.

CUEFL, FCE and CPE in June and December.

DES, CEELT and CEFLS in June only.

Candidates number approximately 200,000 per year.

Yardsticks Chapter 5: 1 2 3 4 5 6 7 8 11 14 17 20

Additionally for DES: 16 19

and for CEFLS: 9 12 15

6.4 City and Guilds
City and Guilds of London Institute

(a) Communication Skills

(b) Communication in Technical English

Purpose

(a) To assess proficiency in a range of Communication Skills in vocational, educational and social contexts.

(b) To assess proficiency in Communication in Technical English including reading, writing and graphical skills.

Elements

Level	*Read*	*Write*	*Listen*	*Speak*	*Time*
(a) I	•	•	•	•	
II	•	•	•	•	course work
III	•	•	•	•	assessment
(b)	•	•			4 hr (2x2 hr)

Content

(a) The assessment of Communication Skills is based on course work designed by the centre, and assignments set by City and Guilds. Students are required to demonstrate through this work that they have the necessary communication skills of reading, listening, writing and speaking to cope with a variety of real or realistic situations ranging from the everyday and familiar at Level I to the complex and public at Level III.

(b) The Communication in Technical English examination requires students to read with understanding simple straightforward prose set in relevant contexts of education, training or work; write effectively in well-constructed sentences on familiar topics; produce and interpret simple sketches, diagrams and charts. It is particularly suitable for those preparing for, or employed in, the construction, engineering and associated industries.

Results

(a) Success is reported in the following units at the highest level achieved.

Reading - receiving and interpreting information in written form
Writing - communicating effectively in written and graphical forms
Speaking - communicating effectively in oral form

Full Level I, II or II certification is met by candidates passing simultaneously or separately the four units of accreditation at the same level, or at a higher level.

(b) Certificates are awarded to those successful in the Understanding and Written papers showing Pass, Credit or Distinction grades in each paper.

C & G	ESU Level
(a) Level I	4
II	6
III	7
(b) Pass	6

*361 Communication Skills replaces 772 and 362 Communication Skills with first assessments available in December 1988. The ESU Levels assigned have therefore not yet been verified. The level assigned to Communication in Technical English is approximate since graphical skills and some technical knowledge are included in the assessment.

Availability

(a) Available in Britain and Ireland only. There are around 50,000 candidates each year

(b) Available worldwide at approved centres. There are around 800 candidates each year.

Special Features

(a) The emphasis on centre-designed course work in Communication Skills allows assessment to be based on activities which are relevant to each individual student.

(b) The Communication in Technical English examination is one of the few in this field.

Yardsticks Chapter 5: (a) 1 2 3 4 5 6 7 8 11 14 17

(b) 1 3 6 7 16 19

6.5 English Speaking Board

Oral Assessments in Spoken English as an Acquired Language

Purpose To assess the spoken English of candidates for whom English is not a native language. Emphasis is on the lively use of speech in communication.

Elements

Level	*Read*	*Listen*	*Speak*	*Time*
Foundation (1-3)	•	•	•	6-12 min
Intermediate (1-3)	•	•	•	12-13 min
Advanced (1-3)	•	•	•	30-40 min
Certificate	•	•	•	60 min

Content Personal, face-to-face use of English including group discussion. Attention given to the candidates' cultural backgrounds and personal interests.

Task requirements at all levels (varying in degree of difficulty and timing):

At Foundation Level

1 A prepared talk on a subject of candidate's own choice.

2 Question/answer session on the talk with assessor and listening group.

3 Prepared reading aloud - communication of written word.

At Intermediate Level - in addition to 1-3 above:

4 An impromptu everyday situation is resolved.

At Advanced Level - in addition to 1-4 above:

5 Understanding and exploring a passage read to the candidate.

6 Reading aloud at sight.

At Certificate Level - in addition to 1-6 above:

7 Two prepared talks are required - one vocational and one non-vocational.

8 Presenting and discussing some aspect of the English Speaking World.

Results Certificates at the appropriate level are given to successful candidates and a report with individual advice. Unsuccessful candidates receive a personal report. ESU equivalences have not yet been verified but are believed to be:

ESB		**ESU Level**
Foundation	1	2
Intermediate	1	4
Advanced	1	6
Certificate	Pass	7+

Availability Mainly in Britain, although arrangements can be made for overseas assessment. Approximately 1,000 candidates per year are currently tested. Dates for examination by arrangement.

Yardsticks Chapter 5: 1 2 3 4 5 6

Certificate only: 11 or 12

6.6 Institute of Linguists

English as a Foreign Language

Purpose To assess proficiency in using languages for realistic purposes and using authentic integrated materials. The Institute's English Language examinations form part of a larger programme of examinations set on a common syllabus format, and covering the whole range of languages examined by the Institute.

Elements

Level		*Read*	*Write*	*Listen*	*Speak*	*Time*
Preliminary Certificate		•	x	•	•	1 hr 15 min
General Certificate		•	x	•	•	1 hr 45 min
Advanced Certificate						
Module	A	•	x*	•	•	2 hours
	B	x*	x	•	•	1 hour
	C	•	•	x	x	2 hr 30 min
	D	•	x*	x	x	2 hr 30 min
	E	•	x*	•	•	1 hour
Intermediate Diploma		•	x*	•	•	2 weeks + 2 hours
Diploma						
Module	I	•	x*	•	•	2 weeks + 3 hours
	II	•	x	•	•	2 weeks + 1 hour
	III	•	•	x	x	3 hours
(translation)	IV	•	x*	x	x	3 hours
(interpreting)	V	x	x	•	•	40 minutes
Background Knowledge		x	•	x	x	3 hours

* An asterisk indicates that the skill is exercised in the candidate's L1, and not in English.

Note: In the modular Advanced Certificate and Diploma examinations, candidates have to choose three modules from the 5 on offer.

Content Tasks at the various levels include:

Understanding of authentic documents, signs, instructions and messages, and at the higher levels, memoranda, articles, official and business documents. Authentic listening materials at natural speed such as announcements and messages. In oral interaction, role play encounters with native speakers. The modular tests at the higher levels involve variously, researching and reporting on a topic both in speech and writing; oral interaction for work-related purposes; researching and producing written reports on topics using a wide variety of sources; and using the telephone and producing a written report. At Diploma level there are, in addition: presenting and arguing a case, translating and interpreting.

Results Given at each level as Pass or Fail with a Distinction for work of outstanding quality. ESU equivalents, which have not yet been verified, are believed to be:

IOL	ESU Level
Preliminary Certificate	3
General Certificate	4
Advanced Certificate	6+
Intermediate Diploma	7
Diploma	8

Special Features The examinations are task-based, testing a wide range of language skills in authentic contexts. At all levels the focus is on mediation between English and the candidate's first language.

Revisions The tests described replace the old IOL examinations from 1990 onwards.

Availability Anywhere in the world by arrangement with the British Council's local offices. For dates of sessions contact the Institute. At present the EFL examinations are taken by about 1,000 candidates per year.

Yardsticks Chapter 5: 1 2 3 4 5 6 7 9 12 15 18

6.7 London University
University of London School Examinations Board

(a) 'O' Level English Language, Syllabus B

(b) Certificate of Attainment in English (Laboratory and Non-Laboratory versions)

Purpose

(a) To assess proficiency in standard written English of an international kind.

(b) To form a series of graded tests based on realistic tasks relevant to the candidate's own experience, with separate versions either with a language laboratory or without.

Elements

	Level	*Read*	*Write*			*Time*
(a)	'O'	•	•			3 hr
(b)	**Laboratory**	*Read*	*Write*	*Listen*	*Speak*	
	1		•		•	45 min
	2		•		•	45 min
	3		•		•	1 hr
	4	•	•	•	•	1 hr 30 min
	5	•	•	•	•	1 hr 45 min
	6	•	•	•	•	2 hr
	Non-Laboratory					
	1		•	•		1 hr
	2		•	•		1 hr 10 min
	3		•	•		1 hr 30 min
	4	•	•	•		1 hr 50 min
	5	•	•	•		2 hr
	6	•	•	•		2 hr 30 min

Content

(a) General topics on personal experience and everyday events.

(b) Topics on students' own experience in a sustained context of related events.

Item formats are as follows:

(a) Reading passages with questions - to show attention to detail (including usage and idiom), the selection and ordering of information and the writing of extended responses based on the texts or according to given guidelines.

(b) Listening to speakers and transferring information, organizing information on diagrams, responding to and asking recorded questions, using graphic and verbal material for oral and written response. Giving a talk on a topic from the test. Producing continuous writing on the test theme assisted by visual materials; writing a letter or report.

Results

(a) Performance is assessed in six grades, A, B or C (corresponding to the former GCE 'O' level pass), D, E and Unclassified.

(b) Certificates are given on a Pass/Fail basis and descriptors of achievement at all levels are provided. ESU Level equivalents, which have not yet been statistically verified, are believed to be:

London University	ESU Level	London University
(a)		(b)
	2+	1
	3+	2
	5	3
Grade 'C'	6	4
	6+	5
	7+	6

Special Features The new Certificate of Attainment, based on the principle of graded testing, is related to learning experiences and to realistic tasks. There is an option of using the language laboratory for the examination.

Availability Worldwide at approved centres in (a) January and June and (b) March, May, July, September and December. The present number of candidates examined per year is approximately 55,000.

Yardsticks Chapter 5: (a) 1 3 6 7 20

(b) 1 2 3* 4 5 6* 7* 8 11 14* 15* 17 (* not Grades 1-3)

6.8 Trinity College London

Spoken English for Speakers of Other Languages

Purpose To assess at all levels the candidates' oral communication skills - understanding spoken English and speaking it communicatively.

Elements

Levels	*Read*	*Listen/Speak*	*Time*
Grades 1 to 3		•	5-7 mins
Grades 4 to 8	•	•	8-15 mins
Grades 9 to 12	•	•	20-50 mins

Note: There is provision for a writing element at Grades 11 and 12.

Content The topics range from everyday greetings and well-known facts to discussion on prepared books and topics concerned with the candidate's studies, occupation and general interests. The tasks, which are set in a face-to-face interview, are very varied over the twelve grades, but here are some typical examples.

At the lower grades: Exchanging greetings, responding to commands and answering short questions. Describing familiar operations, eg cleaning teeth. The asking of questions by the candidate. Telling the examiner about a short reading passage.

At the middle grades: Speaking a part from a dialogue involving filling the blanks left. Discussing the plot and characters of a book; and conversation.

At the higher grades: Discussing up to three books, giving a prepared talk or story for up to 5 minutes. Re-telling a heard passage and answering questions on it, and reporting a heard passage in writing from notes.

Results Certificates are awarded for each of the twelve grades at Pass, Merit, Honours. Written reports are given on the candidates' performance. ESU equivalences have been estimated as:

TCL	**ESU Level**
12	8
11	7
10	6
8 and 9	5
6 and 7	4
4 and 5	3
2 and 3	2+
1	2

Special Features Careful gradation of levels in face-to-face assessment. Emphasis on personal, face-to-face oral interaction.

Revisions The syllabus is being revised and there may be a reduction in the number of grades.

Availability In Britain and overseas through centres in Europe, Middle East, India and Sri Lanka, Far East, Australia, New Zealand and South America. Number of candidates examined annually is about 27,000.

Yardsticks Chapter 5: 1 3 4 5 20 21

Upper Grades: 7 and 11 or 12

6.9 National Board
National Board of Speech and Drama Studies

English as a Foreign Language

Purpose To assess the ability of candidates to communicate effectively in spoken English where the emphasis is on authentic interviews.

Elements

Stage	*Read*	*Listen*	*Speak*	*Time*
1 and 2		•	•	8-10 min
3 to 7	•	•	•	12-25 min

Content The topics used are familiar ones such as home, school, hobbies, occupation and matters of current concern. The test tasks include: Prepared talks of an informal kind, responses to written texts to test the understanding of facts and of underlying intentions and responses to picture stimuli. Responses to authentic listening material by discussion and expressing of language notions conveyed in the material. There is also an opportunity for role-playing.

Results Given in seven levels: elementary, 1 and 2; intermediate, 3 and 4; advanced 5 to 7. ESU Level equivalents, not yet verified, are believed to be:

NBSD	ESU Level
1	2
2	3
3	4
4	5
5	6
6	7
7	7+

Special Features The National Board examinations emphasise oral communication in authentic, face-to-face settings.

Revisions The examination described above is a completely revised form of the earlier Board examinations. The new format is in use from 1989.

Availability In Britain and elsewhere, mainly in Europe. Candidates numbers are approximately 1,000 per year.

Yardsticks Chapter 5: 1 2 3 4 5 6 21

6.10 Pitman Examinations Institute

(a) English for Speakers of Other Languages

(b) English for Business Communications

Purpose

(a) General test of English for speakers of other languages.

(b) Test of skills in using English in business communication; for native speakers, and for overseas students with a fair command of English.

Elements

	Level	*Read*	*Write*	*Listen*	*Time*
(a)	Basic	•	•	•	2 hr
	Elementary	•	•	•	2 hr
	Intermediate	•	•	•	2 hr 30 min
	Hr. Intermediate	•	•	•	2 hr 30 min
	Advanced	•	•	•	3 hr
(b)	Elementary		•		2 hr
	Intermediate		•		2 hr 30 min
	Advanced		•		3 hr

Content

(a) The topics are taken from general, everyday situations. The test items cover:

Listening: choosing the best of four options given; matching spoken with written choices. Task completion with maps, diagrams and tables. Changing messages from spoken to written form. Usage: completing blanks and choosing options. Reading: text structure, reconstruction of texts matching what is written to pictures and any other visual information, scanning texts to extract specific information, questions on a text, task completion using maps, diagrams, tables. Writing: tasks testing candidates ability to follow format, style and topic given in a text, and compositions from a range of topics.

(b) Topics require a knowledge of business practice and related correspondence. Items include:

A gap-filling, objective test. Writing letters, memoranda, telegrams, reports and advertisements from information given.

Results Expressed as Pass (60%) or Fail; there is a First Class Pass (75%) at the Intermediate to Advanced levels. 'Weakness slips' are provided for candidates who fail. Equivalences to ESU Levels are calculated as:

Pitman		**ESU Level**
(a) ESOL	(b) Business	
Basic	-	2+
Elementary	-	3+
Intermediate	Elementary	5
Hr. Intermediate	-	6
-	Intermediate	6+
Advanced	-	7
-	Advanced	7+

Special Features A series of general and business English examinations available worldwide on demand. There are also examinations in English for the Secretary and English for Office Skills testing elements of English knowledge or skill with particular reference to the needs of young office workers.

Revisions The ESOL Examination is a new one, introduced in 1988. Further changes may be announced.

Availability Worldwide at any time of the year at dates arranged by a large number of overseas examination centres. The annual number of candidates for the examinations is about 50,000 general English and 24,000 business English (EBC and EOS).

Yardsticks Chapter 5: (a) 1 2 3 4 5 6 14 17 20

(b) 1 3 7 18 20

6.11 London Chamber of Commerce
London Chamber of Commerce Examinations Board

(a) English for Commerce

(b) English for Business

(c) Spoken English for Commerce and Industry

Purpose To assess the ability to use written and spoken English effectively in commercial or business contexts.

Elements

Levels	*Read*	*Write*	*Speak*	*Time*
(a) for Commerce, (b) for Business.				
First	•	•		2 hr
Second	•	•	•	(a) 2 hr (b) 2 hr 30 min
Third	•	•	•	3 hr

Levels	*Read*	*Write*	*Listen*	*Speak*	*Time*
(c) Spoken English					
Preliminary			•	•	20 min
Threshold	•		•	•	27-35 min
Intermediate	•	•	•	•	30-35 min
Advanced	•	•	•	•	45-50 min

Note: The examinations in English for Commerce and for Business are separate examinations covering business and office tasks. They are mainly distinguished by the way language is elicited and the importance attached to communication in business formats.

Content The Commerce and Business tasks include at the appropriate levels:

Writing on a selected topic, writing a letter and showing understanding of a passage by short answers, writing a summary of an extended passage. Conducting a conversation with the examiner. In the Business examination, in addition, questions are asked on diagrams or numerical tables; business documents and forms are used for comprehension.

The Spoken examination includes:

Having a conversation on general topics and developing themes, responding to instructions, describing a picture or series of pictures and role-playing. The listening element involves interpreting pictures and diagrams, pathfinding and summarising a passage, having taken notes on the basis of a cassette recording. A specially-chosen topic is presented by the candidate and discussed intensively at Advanced level and is available as an additional option at Intermediate level.

Results (a) and (b) Certificates are granted for each level tested, 50% being required for a Pass and 75% for a Distinction. For (c), a results slip shows the performance on five factors on a ten-point scale, a Pass being represented by a Distinction, Credit or Satisfactory grading. The ESU Level equivalents are estimated as follows:-

LCC (a & b)	ESU Level	LCC (c)	ESU Level
First Level	3+	Preliminary	3
Second Level	6	Threshold	5
Third Level	7	Intermediate	6
		Advanced	7

Special Features Specially designed for use by those concerned with Commerce and Industry. The Spoken English examination is, especially at the higher levels, an extended scrutiny of oral proficiency in a business or commercial context. Flexible arrangements are possible for both location and time of examining. The LCC examinations are taken by approximately 28,000 candidates per year.

Availability (a) Worldwide in May, June and November; and also March for First and Second levels. (b) Worldwide in May, June/July and November/December. (c) In UK and Europe; elsewhere by negotiation at any agreed time of the year.

Yardsticks Chapter 5: (a) 1 2* 3 5* 6 7 12* 15 18 (* not First level)

(b) 1 2* 3 5* 6 7 12* 15 18 (* not First level)

(c) 1 2 3* 4 5 6* 7* 9 12 (* not Preliminary or Threshold level)

6.12 AEB
Associated Examining Board

Test in English for Educational Purposes (TEEP)

Purpose To assess the ability of overseas students applying for further and higher education in Britain to carry out their studies in English.

Elements

Read	*Write*	*Listen*	*Speak (optional)*	*Time*
•	•	•	•	4 hr 45 min

Content The topics are those likely to be covered on an educational course without being too specialised. There are alternative papers for subjects with a science/engineering focus and for those on the arts/social/business studies orientation. Parts of the test examine the lecture and seminar situations. There is also an optional spoken section. The first paper covers reading followed by short answer and summary questions; writing down what is said in a recording; listening to a taped lecture, taking notes and then using the notes to answer questions on the lecture and to write a summary of it.

The second paper presents a reading text followed by gap-filling and short answer items; a recorded interview from which candidates take notes and give written answers to questions; the writing of summaries from notes and correcting a short passage containing errors.

The spoken assessment is carried out in a language laboratory in which the candidates speak about themselves, respond to remarks made, answer questions on a taped discussion, respond to questions based on charts, diagrams and graphs and prepare answers from verbal and numerical information.

Results A profile is given of the candidate's proficiency in the areas tested. The results are graded from 0 to 4, covering beginner level needing long-term language tuition, to full proficiency for studies. ESU Level equivalents, which have not yet been verified, are believed to be:

AEB	ESU Level
1	3+
2	5
3	6
4	7

Special Features Specially devised for those with academic requirements in English and based on close study of the language problems they are likely to meet.

Availability In Britain in January/February, May and September. The annual number of candidates at present being tested is 1,000.

Yardsticks Chapter 5: 1 2 3 4 5* 6 7 10 16 19 (* optional)

6.13 ELTS

The English Language Testing Service of the British Council and Cambridge Syndicate

Purpose: To provide a systematic and continuously available system of assessing the English-language proficiency of non-native speakers who intend to study or train in the medium of English.

Elements

Module	*Read*	*Write*	*Listen*	*Speak*	*Time*
Academic	•	•	•	•	3 hr
Non-academic	•	•	•	•	1 hr 30 min

Content

Academic Test
The topics are those likely to be met with in further study or training. There are five sub-tests; two of these are designed to test general English ability and the other three form modules to test language skills in particular subject areas. The general part of the test consists of a test of reading which tests a candidate's general proficiency and general ability on a variety of non-specialist texts and a listening test, based on tape recordings. For the reading test, the skills tested include understanding conceptual meaning, understanding relations within the sentence and scanning to locate specific meaning. For the listening test, identifying figures and diagrams from short descriptions, listening for specific information in an interview, replying to questions and responding to prómpts in a seminar situation are among skills tested.

The modular part of the test contains three subject-specific sub-tests. For each subject area there is a Source Booklet containing a variety of extracts from appropriate articles, reports, tables etc. The tests are 'Study Skills' which test the candidate's ability to handle material in a broad subject area relevant to their own field or study through intensive and extensive reading, separating fact from opinion and interpreting graphs, etc; 'Writing' which requires candidates to carry out two writing tasks based on the Source Booklet, one note-taking and the other a connected piece of writing; and 'Interview' which is conducted by a qualified and trained assessor and included an extended discussion based on one of the sections in the Source Booklet and discussion of future plans with regard to study or training programmes.

Non-academic training module
The Non-academic training module is intended for candidates whose training is to be of a practical or technical nature. The test lasts 1 1/2 hours and is made up of the following sub-tests:

Listening	30 minutes
Reading and Writing	45 minutes
Interview	15 minutes

Results

i) Levels of performance for various courses have been worked out, eg Bands 6/7 would be widely acceptable for University studies.

ii) Guidance may also be gained about the amount of language tuition needed for a candidate to reach a required level, should tuition be seen to be required.

ELTS	ESU Level
1	2/1
2	2+
3	3+
4	4
5	5
6	6
7	7
8	8
9	8/9

Special Features The ELTS test has been specially designed to assess linguistic readiness for academic studies, and also has a non-academic component. Officially accepted by all universities in the UK and a growing number in Australia and North America. Conducted in conjunction with the Cambridge Syndicate.

Revisions As a result of validation studies and extensive consultation over the past three or four years, ELTS is being revised, although maximum continuity will be sought in its future structure. Piloting and trialling have been carried out and the new test is available from autumn 1989.

Availability Available under the auspices of the British Council at over 150 centres in more than 100 countries worldwide, including nine centres in the UK. In 1987/88 the test was administered to over 15,000 candidates. Test dates are flexible and relate to local conditions in the countries concerned; the test can be given on demand by arrangement with the local British Council office.

Yardsticks Chapter 5: 1 2 3 4 5 6 7 10 13 16 19 20

6.14 Joint Matriculation Board

University Entrance Test in English for Speakers of Other Languages

Purpose To assess whether candidates intending to study for a degree have sufficient English for studying in the medium of English.

Elements

Read	*Write*	*Listen*	*Speak*	*Time*
•	•	•	•	3 hr 40 min

Content The topics are those likely to be needed by university students, especially those studying the physical or social sciences. Test tasks include:

Descriptive writing: description or report on a process or procedure, an instruction for a simple technical task based on written or graphic information.

Discursive writing: an extended piece of writing, interpreting extended graphic or written information. Editing through a cloze test, correction of texts and matching dictionary definitions with text items. Reading: text-handling tasks using an academic text. Listening comprehension: using a range of skills, of taped lectures or discussions, responses in short answers or by table completion. Speaking: an interview, first an informal discussion and then a more formal treatment of a topic chosen by the candidate.

Results Pass/fail on a scale of A to D using a profile of the five skill areas tested. Candidates require a minimum of two C's and three higher grades to pass. ESU Level equivalents are:

JMB	**ESU Level**
Pass	6

Special Features This is an advanced examination for University entrance purposes. It covers language skills identified as necessary for degree studies.

Availability Available in Britain and overseas in March and June. At present it is held mainly in Britain and currently tests about 5,000 students per year.

Yardsticks Chapter 5: 1 2 3 4 5 6 7 10 13 16 19 20

6.15 North Western Advisory Council

North Western Regional Advisory Council for Further Education

Examination in English as a Second Language

Purpose To assess proficiency in factual, or 'transactional' English as it is used in schools for day-to-day purposes at a level sufficient to cope with secondary examinations.

Elements

Level	*Read*	*Write*	*Listen*	*Speak*	*Time*
Intermediate	•	•	•	•	5 hr 15 min

Note: Basic and Advanced level tests are in preparation.

Content The content of the proposed Basic and Advanced tests has not yet been finalised. Here is that for the Intermediate examination. The topics focus on factual matters - reports, instructions, accounts of a semi-academic kind rather than on topics of social, or interactional, English. The test tasks include:

Continuous writing in response to non-verbal information in graphs, tables, diagrams, etc. Reading comprehension with responses such as labelling diagrams, re-ordering a summary and completing written responses. Cloze testing of grammatical forms. Listening to a taped talk and responding by labelling diagrams and re-ordering statements. Making spoken responses in set situations, responses being recorded for teacher and central assessment.

Results The skills are assessed separately and a profile report is prepared at Pass, Credit, Distinction and Ungraded levels. Candidates may sit examinations in individual skills at different levels. ESU Level equivalents are not yet verified but believed to be:

NWRAC	**ESU Level**
Basic	3
Intermediate	5
Advanced	7

Special Features The focus of the examination is on handling factual, transactional information related to secondary-school studies.

Revisions Basic and Advanced level examinations are in preparation and the opening of overseas centres is proposed.

Availability For students in British secondary schools and further education colleges. Held in Britain only (at present) between March and May each year. The number of candidates per year is approximately 1,000.

Yardsticks Chapter 5: 1 2 3 4 5 6 7 10 13 16 19 20

Chapter 7
Choosing the Right Examination

We have now given much of the information you will need to make a choice among the available English Language examinations. In this chapter we will go through the stages to be followed in making this crucial decision.

The first step in making a choice is to be clear in your own mind what you will need to use the language for - there are 'horses for courses' as they say. Language needs will, of course, vary widely from the very specific uses, such as taking a post-graduate course in engineering at a British University, to the very general expectation of improving English for possible future use when meeting English speakers and visiting their countries. Nevertheless, it will save time and trouble later to be as clear as possible about language needs at an early stage. This precaution applies to students and language teachers who share in making decisions about which examination to take, and to academic tutors and training directors who interpret the results of examinations and thus set up expectations for future applicants. Just to take a particular examination because lots of other people are doing so, regardless of its purpose, level or content, is not an economical way to plan one's future.

The first and simplest source of guidance in making the choice is the Chart of Levels which we show and discuss in Chapter 4. If you look at the left side of the chart, you will see the nine levels of language proficiency of the ESU Scale, described in very general terms. And, when you have selected a particular level to be examined in, you can then see which examinations are set at that level. In the middle level of proficiency, between 3 and 7, there is a very large choice because, obviously, this is target area for the majority of candidates. You will also see that some of the certificates awarded cover quite a wide range of proficiency; the Oxford Preliminary Certificate covers ESU Levels 3, 4 and 5, dividing the award into Pass, Credit and Distinction grades. Other Boards have up to two grades for an ESU Level, for example, the Trinity College grades 2 to 9 correspond to the ESU Levels 2 to 5, with two grades per Level. Because of this coverage range, we put the symbol for any particular grade on the Chart at the bottom end of the range - the point where a person just gets that grade. He or she could quite possibly be a little higher but, to save over-complication, we do not record this.

We generally place the symbols at one of two points in any Level; at the bottom or in the middle of the box. Although we have gone to a lot of trouble, by discussing grade placements with the Boards and by statistical verification, there must still be a margin of error and we do not think a more refined method of placement would be justified.

So much for information about level. The next decision is about the areas of use covered by the examinations. Looking across the top of the Chart from left to right, we can see three main divisions, from General/Social through Business to Study/Training English. The general descriptors given in the Chart are no longer detailed enough to help us in our choice. We need more precise guidance about the examination's purpose and content. This we will find from the examination particulars in Chapter 6 and the Yardsticks in

Chapter 5. We can then weed out the skills and activities we do not need and focus on those we do need.

It is not necessary, of course, for every candidate to perform equally well in all the four skills shown in the Stage III Yardsticks or to be equally concerned with all the activities shown in those at Stage IV. Furthermore, in some cases, the needs and expectations in English are described in terms of what we call 'enabling skills'. These may be linguistic aspects such as those of grammar (verb tenses, subject-object, pronouns, etc.); lexis (size and range of vocabulary); or discourse (use of cohesion, style, register). Or they may concern functional aspects (instructing, agreeing, persuading) or concepts (such as certainty, possibility, comparison). In addition, examinations require the use of test-taking skills and a facility in handling various test formats. The Yardsticks in Chapter 5 are a veritable mine of information on these many aspects of examination content and technique.

When we have made decisions about Level and Test Coverage, we can turn to the administrative aspects given in the lower half of the Chart - the 'where', 'when' and 'how' details which will guide our choice of examination. It is at this stage that direct contact with the Boards, using the addresses and phone numbers at the bottom of the Chart or in Appendix B, may become necessary. As a general rule, wherever you are, the local office of the British Council, whose Headquarters are in London, is a guaranteed source of information about English examinations - and about any other aspect of English Language teaching you may be interested in.

A simplified diagram for those who need further guidance in choosing examinations is to be found in Figure 7.1. This will help you to 'Find your way through the English Language Examinations Maze'. This diagram, we think, explains itself.

Here are two case studies which may usefully take you through this decision-making process.

Case Study One

A student from Thailand has studied English at school for five years. She has some proficiency in the language but now has a chance of studying Physics at a British Polytechnic and does not think she could really follow such a programme in English with any degree of confidence. What does she do now?

The first step is to make a rough estimate of her present standard of English; five years of classroom English may not mean very much in terms of practical proficiency as many people know to their cost. Either by herself, or perhaps more wisely with her tutor, she looks at the general ESU Scale on the Chart of Levels starting from the bottom. She can see that she is certainly above Levels 1, 2 and 3. She might possibly be at Level 5, but thinks that she is a bit rusty in English and settles for Level 4 - which in essence means that she can just tackle tasks of moderate difficulty but will tend to have communication problems even there.

The second step is to decide the sort of proficiency level needed for her studies. Obviously, taking a course at Polytechnic level will involve tasks of considerable difficulty - studying difficult text books, listening to extended lectures, taking part in experimental workshops and writing assignments and examination papers. It looks as if she should aim for proficiency at or about ESU Level 7.

Figure 7.1 Find your way through the English Language examinations maze (for more detailed information about examinations at each level, see figure 4.1)

You need English for ...?	**BUSINESS**	**GENERAL/ SOCIAL**	**STUDY/ TRAINING**
Higher Studies and the Professions? **Levels 7 to 9**	See **Business English** examinations at ESU Levels 7 to 9	See **General/Social English** examinations at ESU Levels 7 to 9	See **Study/ Training English** examinations at ESU Levels 7 to 9
Moderately useful level of communication? **Levels 4 to 6**	See **Business English** examinations at ESU Levels 4 to 6	See **General/Social English** examinations at ESU Levels 4 to 6	See **Study/ Training English** examinations at ESU Levels 4 to 6
For simple travel and social needs? **Levels 2 and 3**		See **General/Social English** examinations at ESU Levels 2 and 3	

The third step is to choose the most suitable examination for a Physics course at Level 7. As an overseas student, there are three main choices open to her: the Associated Examining Board, Level 4; the English Language Testing Service, at Band 7; and the Joint Matriculation Board University Entrance Examination. From Chapter 6, she finds that the ELTS has a testing module covering Science subjects. She also finds that the British Council in Bangkok gives the ELTS test at regular intervals.

The final step is to find out from the British Council how to prepare for the test, either at home or in Britain depending on the award of a scholarship, and to prepare for her studies and examination in English.

It should be noted that other examinations are also acceptable for higher studies, such as those of the Universities of Cambridge, Oxford and London. One can judge their relative suitability by studying the information available in Chapter 6.

Case Study Two

A young man who has just finished secondary school in Brazil wishes to spend some time visiting relatives in America and Britain before applying for a job with an international airline in Brazil. He has never been particularly good at, or interested in, English but knows a little of the language. He would like to improve his English both to enjoy his visits more and also to increase his chances of getting the airline job. What should he do now?

Again, it is best to tackle the steps mentioned in Case Study One, the first of which is to make an estimate of present standards in English. The young man knows a few greetings and common phrases and can ask for and understand simple directions. He can read very simple sentences but his writing is poor. He would be approximately at Level 3 in oral skills, but below that in the graphic skills. Still, his future language needs are mainly on the conversational side so the graphic skills will not be so important. For his forthcoming travels, he will be able to manage at about Level 4. For the airline job, he would be expected to use the phone and talk to people in the reception area, involving oral skills at Level 5 or 6. He sees that he has a wide choice of examination target: the ARELS Preliminary Certificate at V.Good Pass level; the RSA Intermediate, Listening and Oral; the London Chamber of Commerce, Spoken English, Threshold; the National Board at Level 4; Trinity College at Grade 8, amongst others. Some Boards provide an examination at this level but require an equal level of spoken and written skills so they are not so appropriate for him. For the final choice, much will depend on the availability of the examination in Brazil and the precise content of the tests. A study of the Chart details and the Yardsticks in Chapter 5 plus direct contact with the Boards will cover this area.

These case studies illustrate the kinds of decision needed, the steps to be taken and the sources of information now available to help in making those decisions.

Chapter 8
The Acceptability of Language Certificates

When one has gained a certificate of language proficiency, it is important to know its value. Who accepts it and for what levels? We have found that the British tradition of academic and local independence is still strong when it comes to interpreting the value of an examination grade as a passport to education or employment. The final decision about acceptability in Universities is usually in the hands of the Head of the Department concerned. He or she may abide by guidelines sent round by the university authorities or may, as desired, delegate the decisions to members of staff. The same situation holds in business organisations where departmental freedom in these selection matters is common. It is, therefore, impossible to make a generally true statement about the acceptability of any certificate of English proficiency; one which will hold in all circumstances - there are too many certificates and too many independent people around.

The academic scene is well described in the British Council publications, such as, 'Acceptability of ELTS in UK Universities and Polytechnics', and 'English Language Requirements in British Educational Institutions' (1985). We see that the average ELTS rating accepted across the many institutions listed in the surveys is Band 6.0. However, we see big variations between institutions and also amongst their departments. Bristol University suggest that a minimum of Band 7.5 in each sub-test is desirable, quite a rigorous standard. Other institutions recommend Band 6.0 and, in one university faculty, it appears that even Band 4.0 would be acceptable.

There are also differences in acceptance levels as between Undergraduate and Post-Graduate courses. Some science and technical departments accept a lower level of language proficiency than do arts and social studies departments, possibly because a good proportion of their communication is carried out by non-language means - figures, symbols, diagrams and so on. In judging test performances, institutions often bear in mind the possibility of remedial English courses either before or during the course of study. For example, at Reading University, applicants at Bands 5 or 5.5 will be given an 11-week course in English; those at level 6, an 8-week course, and so on. At Band 7, applicants will be usually be accepted without language tuition. Some universities, such as Exeter, will provide extended tuition courses in English of up to a year for students with very low standards of English. In other words, there is no general 'pass-mark' but a range of ratings, the value of which depends on a number of circumstances.

Apart from an ELTS test rating, universities may recognise a host of other language qualifications, including the Cambridge Syndicate and the Joint Matriculation Board Certificates and the Test of English as a Foreign Language (used in the United States), to mention but a few.

The picture becomes even more confusing when we move away from the comparatively structured academic scene to the wider fields of business, commerce, the armed forces and the public services. In some of these fields, there is little interest in English testing. In others, especially those with strong multi-national links, English testing is an important facet of personnel management. Unfortunately, our information about this area is very limited and we confess we would need to study it more closely before making firm statements about it. We do, however, have reason to assume that there is no comprehensive and generally-accepted code of practice about English Language standards and examinations and that managers and personnel directors will in all probability be given a good deal of latitude when it comes to assessing English Language proficiency.

Obviously, it would be useful to know much more about this matter of examination acceptability. In the meantime, we put forward a number of questions which should at least clarify the problem areas. We classify these questions under two headings:

Test Factors, focussing on the mechanism, content and structure of the tests or examinations; and Institutional Factors, related to the administrative conditions in those organisations which make use of tests.

Questions about Test Factors

- **What is the meaning of a particular certificate of proficiency in English?** This meaning will cover the aspects of level - what level on a scale, say from 1 up to 9, does this performance represent, and of coverage - what kinds of skill are examined in the test at that level? To be useful here, a language certificate should give a clear and specific statement of the level and coverage of the tests used. These aspects will eventually have to be related to the language demands of a job or course in a process of validation.

- **How stable is the test?** One can reasonably expect the coverage and level of difficulty of an examination set in one year to be closely comparable with those of the same examination taken the following year. The independent assessments of two examiners should agree closely with each other. The performance of a candidate on one occasion should match closely his or her performance on another occasion. We would not, of course, expect 100% agreement between such kinds of rating, but we should be able to use statistical methods to find out how stable a test is. At least we should be able to estimate a 'margin of error' to bear in mind when interpreting test results.

- **What is the shelf-life of the certificate?** Clearly, a certificate given in one year will need critical scrutiny if it is produced by a candidate a decade later as there could well have been an improvement or deterioration in a person's proficiency over the years depending on exposure to the language. Or there could have been significant changes in the content of the test over the years.

- **What is the level of language proficiency needed for job or course success?** University experience suggests that the language demands of courses in Law, Literature or Social Studies are more exacting that those of a course in Technology or Computer Science. Similarly, in Business and Industry, different jobs will pose different demands - a high level salesman or director would need a higher and more flexible command of the language than a book-keeper or computer programmer.

- **How can we estimate what language tuition is needed?** It will help us if the test can show, not only that a candidate has failed to reach the required standard, but also how far he or she has to go in order to reach that standard. For this sort of decision, indices of language aptitude have a part to play.

Questions about Institutional Factors

- **Who in an institution makes the decisions about language proficiency?** In some cases, a central decision on minimum language qualifications may be made and handed down to local staff. In others, guidelines are put forward for local decisions. In yet others, the local managers or heads of department are free to use their own discretion about the language proficiency of candidates. If one can generalise about British practice, it is that there is a strong tendency to leave final decisions to the local manager, possibly with the help of broad guidelines about standards. It is unusual to have a mandatory system laid down from a central point.

- **What is the demand for and supply of candidates for a job or course?** If there are large numbers of applicants, the language requirements can be strictly enforced. If, conversely, applicants are few and badly needed, language requirements will be relaxed and provision will be made for language tuition.

- **What tolerance is there for those with lower language standards?** Sometimes a job or course is so exacting that it would be disastrous, not least for the candidate, to be launched into it without sufficient language preparation. A course in Advanced Economics, for example, intended for a group of native-English speakers would provide a stressful environment for a person with low proficiency in English, left to sink or swim unaided. On the other hand, a specially-organised group of non-native speakers on a course could be given more attention as regards language and be expected to progress at a slower pace. One would also expect the tutors to adjust their language sensitively to their students' level. Again, the pressures of the job itself may also be taken into account. The critical nature of the work of an air-traffic controller or of a senior theatre nurse would rule out the employment of anyone likely to confuse or misinterpret language instructions.

There are, as we have implied, several avenues which can be followed up. The starting point has been to clarify the levels and content of a range of language examinations so that performance in any one examination can be clearly described on a common framework. But setting up the framework of description is only a beginning. When we have gained experience in using it with the Examining Boards and close contacts with users in Education and Business, we should be able to build up a data base for validating the whole decision-making system. It might then be possible for user groups to be more positive about issuing central guidelines (if not requirements) about the minimum language proficiency requirements and, therefore, examination acceptability for a range of jobs and courses. There should be no reason why, once the 'Framework' concept has been accepted and is seen to be workable, steady progress should not be made towards this goal of harmonisation.

In the light of experience in using the model, it is hoped that Framework will evolve because of changes in examination formats and content and pressure from users for revision.

Chapter 9
Broader Implications of Framework

Our original purpose in devising Framework was to provide a system for describing and comparing English Language examinations. We can also use the Yardsticks and their descriptors to describe learners' language proficiency as indicated by their examination results. As we have seen, the Framework can be extended to include other English Language examinations, revisions of existing examinations and even examinations in other languages.

Because the Framework Yardsticks offer users a comprehensive series of language performance specifications which have been agreed by the major examining bodies, they provide a system which users can apply to other areas of language education. We discuss some of these other uses in the following sections.

Definitions of standards

As a profession, teachers have a terminology for describing stages of attainment which is fairly widely used, including such terms as 'elementary', 'intermediate', 'advanced' and so on. However, these terms are notoriously ill-defined and variable, so that one teacher's 'intermediate' may not be another's, and an 'intermediate' student in, say, Italy may not be regarded as 'intermediate' in India. Alternatively, language levels have been described in terms of the examinations which learners are preparing for or which they have passed. But, as we have seen, these examination levels may mean very little outside a narrow circle and it has been difficult until now to relate the level of one examination to that of another. Framework gives us a means of defining levels of proficiency which is both more useful (because it uses descriptors for its levels) and less open to mis-interpretation (because the levels have been verified) than the traditional terminology.

Defining language course objectives

Language schools have usually defined their course objectives in terms of the duration of the course, some label related to level, or to the grades of a known examination. Using Framework levels to define both the starting and terminal levels of courses will be more precise and should be more universally understood than using the terms of any of these traditional definitions.

Describing course materials

The proficiency levels of textbooks and other language-learning materials have been equally difficult to describe, largely because of the imprecise nature of the terminology used. Using Framework, authors and publishers will be able to describe the proficiency levels at which their books are pitched and the types of learner they are suitable for. And this should be done with much greater precision than is achieved by the many catalogues and blurbs at present in use.

Describing language needs and entry requirements

All too often, potential students are put off applying for British universities because they cannot cope with the complexities of the entry requirements. Different universities state their English-language requirements in different ways, demanding a variety of grades of a number of examinations. Further difficulties arise when they fail to mention a particular qualification which applicants might possess - does this mean that their qualifications are unacceptable? Should they take further examinations just to make sure? Which ones should they take? And what grades must they attain?

Framework should help them in their dilemma, allowing users such as employers and admissions tutors at colleges and universities to describe their language needs and entry requirements in clear, widely-understood terms. So institutions will be able play their part by specifying the content (using particular Yardsticks) and the level (on the 1 to 9 scale) which they expect for a particular job or course. The use of Framework for such placement decisions can be supplemented, with suitable candidates, by its use for self-assessment, possibly with the help of translation into the mother tongue. A major area of weakness at the moment is that all employers and institutions of further and higher education define their requirements using different criteria, different terminology and referring to different examinations. This is not only confusing for students when they are applying for jobs or courses, it is also damaging to the end users who do not get applicants in the numbers and of the quality that they otherwise might.

Framework and modern language teaching

We have sometimes been asked about the value of the Framework descriptions in the field of modern language teaching and testing. This is an important point, which we have borne in mind when devising our model. The fact is that at no place in Framework do we specify any uniquely English language items - the descriptions of level, of difficulty and of performance acceptability are framed wholly in the operational terms relating to the social, occupational or study needs of a person. The descriptors, then, will apply equally to any language used in a situation, whether it be English, Arabic, French, German or any other living language. The actual language in use will vary from occasion to occasion, but the purposes of its use and the performance criteria by which it is judged, being operational, will remain the same whatever the language. In many international companies, for example, the staff switch from language to language according to the demands of the situation. In many countries, school children are prepared to cope with two or more linguistic media. In all these circumstances, the descriptions of Framework will apply to the processes of learning and assessment - they are, as it were, 'language-free'.

Describing overlaps and gaps in examination provision

Framework began as an exercise in language description. Obviously, it can describe only those examinations which existed at the time of making the description. However, because the Framework model places examinations on Yardsticks according to both content and level, it also reveals overlaps and gaps in the present examination provision. Of course, there may well be good reasons for these gaps and overlaps - there is likely to be a number of examinations for which there is a heavy demand, and there is unlikely to be such a demand for examinations in English for Specific Purposes at the lower levels of proficiency, and this is undoubtedly the reason why so few are available. However, when all the main examinations have been included on the Framework, the areas of sparse and dense provision become apparent.

Appendix A
Other EFL Examinations

Some other examinations in English as a Foreign or International Language are:

Educational Testing Service, Princeton, New Jersey which conducts the Test of English as a Foreign Language (TOEFL) and the Test of Spoken English (TSE), the main examinations of this kind in the United States.

English Language Institute of the University of Michigan is responsible for the Michigan English Language Assessment Battery.

English Language Teaching Development Unit, Northants produces the ELTDU Stages of Attainment Scale and Test Battery.

Franco-British Chamber of Commerce and Industry, Paris has examinations in Commercial and Business English, in Commercial English - Hotel and Tourism, and Transport and Logistics.

General Medical Council, London has a test of proficiency in English (PLAB) for medical practitioners.

International Baccalaureate, Geneva has a test in English as a Second Language.

International Certificate Conference, Frankfurt has several tests in English, including English for Business, Hotel and Catering and Technical Purposes.

Language Training Services, Bath has the Business English Test.

There are **Teacher Training qualifications** awarded by the Cambridge Syndicate/Royal Society of Arts, Trinity College London, The English Speaking Board and the College of Preceptors.

For further information about all the above examinations, please consult the *Longman Guide to English Language Examinations.*

Appendix B
Addresses for Framework Project

The Associated Examining Board
South Western Office
Netherton House
23 - 29 Marsh Street
Bristol BS1 4BP (0272) 273434

Association of Recognised English Language Schools
(AET)
Ewert House
Ewert Place
Summertown
Oxford OX2 7BZ (0865) 514272

City and Guilds of London Institute
(C & G)
46 Britannia Street
London WC1X 9RG (01) 278 2468

Brendan J. Carroll
8 Manor Place
Newbury
Berkshire RG13 1RB

English Language Testing Service
The British Council
10 Spring Gardens
London SW1A 2BN (01) 930 8466
and
University of Cambridge Local Examinations Syndicate
Syndicate Buildings
1 Hills Road
Cambridge CB1 2EU (0223) 61111

English Speaking Board (International) Limited
32 Norwood Avenue
Southport
Merseyside PR9 9EG (0704) 231366

The English-Speaking Union of the Commonwealth
Dartmouth House
37 Charles Street
London W1X 8AB (01) 493 3328

Institute of Linguists Examinations Board
Mangold House
24a Highbury Grove
London N5 2EA (01) 359 7445 / 6386

Joint Matriculation Board
(JMB)
Manchester M15 6EU (061) 273 2565

London Chamber of Commerce Examinations Board
Marlowe House
Station Road
Sidcup
Kent DA15 7BJ (01) 302 0261

National Board of Speech and Drama Studies
Jordan House
47 Brunswick Place
London N1 6EE (01) 251 0077

North West Regional Examinations Board
Town Hall
Walkden Road
Worsley
Manchester M28 4QE (061) 702 8700

Pitman Examinations Institute
Godalming
Surrey GU7 1UU (04868) 5311

Trinity College London
11-13 Mandeville Place
London W1M 6AQ (01) 935 5773

University of Cambridge Local Examinations Syndicate and **Royal Society of Arts Examinations Board**
Syndicate Buildings
1 Hills Road
Cambridge CB1 2EU (0223) 61111

University of London School Examinations Board
Stewart House
32 Russell Square
London WC1B 5DN (01) 636 8000

University of Oxford Delegacy of Local Examinations (Oxford)
Ewert House
Ewert Place
Summertown
Oxford OX1 7BZ (0865) 54291

Richard West
University of Manchester
Department of Education
Oxford Road
Manchester M13 9PL (061) 275 3483

Appendix C
Verification Data

In this Appendix, we will give further details of the verification study we carried out to establish the reliability of the examination grade ESU equivalents in the Chart of Levels.

At an early stage in the Framework project , we agreed with the Boards, on a subjective basis, where their various grades appeared to fit the descriptors on the ESU Nine-point Scale. For example, a Board's Elementary, Intermediate and Higher Certificate's might be judged to be at ESU Levels 3, 5 and 7 respectively. Such assessments, made by experienced examiners after full consideration, are no doubt a good guide to standards, but their credibility is greatly improved if supported by objective indices of reliability.

The purpose of the present verification study was to provide this objective support to the subjective estimates. The *first step* was to collect samples of writing and speaking made by candidates of a wide range of proficiency in the Boards' examinations. These samples were rated by a large number of experienced teachers/examiners using the ESU Scales. We then selected the raters with the highest correlations with the overall ratings made by all the judges, on the assumption that the mean ratings of a number of experienced assessors would approach the 'true' grading of the samples. We also selected the writing and speech examples about which our judges showed the greatest agreement, eliminating those examples which gave rise to the greatest rating variation. The revised samples, under different code letters, were then re-submitted for rating on the ESU Scales to the selected judges after an interval of two to three months. In this way, we arrived at a package of 20 writing and 16 speech samples which had each been reliably calibrated in ESU Levels by 10 reliable raters. The median inter- rater and repeat reliabilities were in region of 0.950 as can be seen from the accompanying Table C5.

The *second step* was to send copies of the writing and speech to the Boards who were asked to assess them according to the criteria normally applied in their examinations.

The *third step* was to check the subjective ratings made at an earlier stage in the project against the statistically supported calibrations and to adjust them as necessary. This was done and some adjustments,many of them quite small, were duly made. The levels in the chart show those adjustments for those Boards completing the verification process.

The verification study, which we believe to be the first statistical comparative study of a range of important examinations, produced two main results. First, it provided a firm basis for allocating ESU Levels to the examination grades. Secondly, it ratifies the basic assumption of the Framework project in that all the Boards concerned were able to relate the ESU level definitions to their own rating criteria, thus defusing the 'chalk and cheese' reservations expressed earlier.

For those interested in the statistics, we now give the following details:

- ratings by the judges of the writing and speech samples on the ESU scales. (C1,C3)
- correlation matrices showing inter-correlations of writing and of speech ratings. (C2,C4)
- median and range of correlations of initial, final and repeat ratings. (C5)
- factor structure revealed by Factor Analyses of the correlation matrices. (C6,C7)

Statistical Analyses for Framework Verification
ESU Ratings given for 20 Essays by 10 Raters (C1)

E1	R1	R2	R3	R4	R5	R6	R7	R8	R9	R10	AV	SE
E1	9.0	9.0	9.0	9.0	9.0	9.0	9.0	9.0	9.0	9.0	9.00	.00
E2	8.0	8.0	8.0	7.0	8.0	8.0	8.0	7.5	8.0	8.0	7.85	.11
E3	8.0	7.0	8.0	7.0	8.0	7.5	8.0	7.5	8.0	8.0	7.70	.13
E4	8.0	8.0	6.5	8.0	8.0	7.5	7.0	8.0	7.0	7.5	7.55	.17
E5	7.0	6.0	7.0	6.0	7.0	7.0	7.0	7.5	6.5	7.0	6.80	.15
E6	5.0	6.0	6.0	6.0	7.0	7.0	6.0	5.5	7.0	6.0	6.15	.21
E7	6.0	5.0	7.0	7.0	6.5	5.5	6.0	6.0	7.0	7.5	6.35	.25
E8	7.0	5.0	6.0	6.0	6.0	6.5	6.0	7.0	6.0	6.5	6.20	.19
E9	6.0	6.0	5.0	5.0	6.0	6.0	5.0	7.5	6.0	7.0	5.95	.26
E10	5.0	5.0	5.0	6.0	5.5	4.5	5.0	4.5	5.0	5.5	5.10	.15
E11	6.0	4.0	5.0	4.0	5.0	4.5	5.0	4.5	6.0	5.0	4.90	.22
E12	6.0	4.0	4.0	5.0	6.0	4.5	4.0	4.5	5.0	4.5	4.75	.24
E13	5.0	4.0	4.0	5.0	5.5	4.5	5.0	4.5	4.0	6.0	4.75	.21
E14	5.0	5.0	3.0	4.0	5.0	3.5	3.0	3.5	3.0	4.5	3.95	.27
E15	4.0	3.0	3.0	4.0	3.5	3.5	3.0	4.0	3.0	4.0	3.50	.15
E16	3.0	3.0	3.0	3.0	4.0	3.5	4.0	3.5	4.0	4.0	3.50	.15
E17	3.0	3.0	3.0	3.0	3.0	3.5	3.0	3.0	3.0	4.0	3.15	.11
E18	3.0	3.0	4.0	4.0	3.0	3.5	3.0	2.5	2.0	3.0	3.10	.19
E19	2.0	3.0	3.0	3.0	3.0	3.0	2.0	2.0	2.0	2.5	2.55	.16
E20	2.0	2.0	2.0	2.0	2.0	2.0	2.0	2.0	2.0	2.0	2.00	.00
AV	5.4	5.0	5.0	5.2	5.6	5.2	5.1	5.2	5.2	5.6	5.24	-
SE	.47	.44	.47	.39	.44	.44	.46	.48	.49	.44	-	-

Correlation Matrix for 10 Essay Raters (C2)
(Decimal points omitted)

	1	2	3	4	5	6	7	8	9	10
2	906									
3	894	895								
4	904	916	927							
5	947	947	917	941						
6	914	947	951	920	952					
7	923	912	967	919	949	965				
8	941	914	901	894	927	954	933			
9	914	889	942	890	948	943	962	924		
10	931	913	925	924	948	936	954	958	940	
ALL	959	954	963	953	979	980	980	967	967	975

ESU Levels given for 16 Oral Interviews by 10 Raters (C3)

	R1	R2	R3	R4	R5	R6	R7	R8	R9	R10	AV	SE
O1	8.0	8.5	8.0	8.5	8.0	8.0	9.0	9.0	9.0	9.0	8.50	.15
O2	8.0	8.0	7.0	8.5	8.0	8.0	8.0	8.0	8.0	8.0	7.95	.12
O3	7.5	8.0	7.5	7.0	7.0	7.0	8.0	7.0	7.0	7.0	7.30	.13
O4	7.0	6.0	6.0	6.0	7.0	8.0	7.5	7.0	6.0	7.0	6.75	.23
O5	6.5	7.5	7.0	6.0	6.0	7.0	7.0	6.0	5.5	6.5	6.50	.20
O6	6.0	6.0	5.0	7.0	6.0	7.0	7.0	6.0	5.0	6.0	6.10	.23
O7	7.0	6.5	5.0	7.5	6.5	5.0	5.5	6.0	5.0	5.5	5.95	.28
O8	5.5	6.0	5.0	6.0	6.0	5.0	5.5	5.0	4.0	5.0	5.30	.20
O9	5.0	6.0	4.0	5.0	7.0	7.0	5.0	5.0	5.0	5.0	5.40	.31
O10	5.0	5.0	5.0	6.0	6.5	6.0	4.0	4.0	4.0	5.0	5.05	.28
O11	6.0	6.0	4.0	6.0	5.0	5.0	6.0	4.0	4.0	5.0	5.10	.28
O12	5.0	5.0	5.0	5.0	4.0	4.0	6.0	4.0	5.0	4.0	4.70	.21
O13	5.0	4.0	4.0	5.0	4.0	4.0	4.0	4.0	4.0	4.0	4.20	.13
O14	3.0	4.0	2.0	3.0	4.0	3.0	4.0	2.0	3.0	4.0	3.20	.25
O15	2.0	3.0	2.0	4.0	2.0	2.0	3.0	2.0	3.0	2.0	2.50	.22
O16	3.0	2.0	2.0	2.0	2.0	2.0	2.0	2.0	3.0	2.0	2.20	.13
AV	5.6	5.7	4.9	5.7	5.6	5.5	5.7	5.1	5.1	5.3	5.42	-
SE	.45	.47	.47	.46	.45	.52	.49	.52	.44	.48	-	-

Correlation Matrix for 10 Oral Interview Raters (C4)
(Decimal points omitted)

	1	2	3	4	5	6	7	8	9	10
2	927									
3	924	939								
4	921	913	876							
5	895	914	861	903						
6	870	885	862	826	944					
7	921	930	919	859	829	878				
8	952	927	937	920	904	898	941			
9	870	873	899	835	817	816	901	948		
10	946	947	940	906	922	932	958	966	927	
ALL	965	968	958	936	941	934	956	983	929	988

Comparison of Initial, Final and Repeat Rating Correlations (C5)

Initial correlations of 35 raters with mean rating. Median 0.910, range 0.533 to 0.975
Final correlations of 14 raters with mean ratings. Median 0.964, range 0.929 to 0.988
Repeat correlations of 11 raters on same texts. Median 0.955, range 0.877 to 0.971

Factor Analysis of Essay Ratings by 10 Raters (C6)
(Decimal points omitted)

	Orthogonal solution		Oblique solution	
	Factor 1	Factor 2	Factor 1	Factor 2
1	955	078	730	238
2	956	207	999	- 161
3	962	- 206	- 141	999
4	954	- 001	487	480
5	973	053	663	323
6	962	065	694	281
7	981	- 136	084	910
8	957	152	958	012
9	964	- 160	001	977
10	970	- 047	354	629
Var'ce	98.2%	1.8%	74.2%	25.8%

Factor Analysis of Oral Ratings by 10 Raters (C7)
(Decimal points omitted)

	Orthogonal solution		Oblique solution	
	Factor 1	Factor 2	Factor 1	Factor 2
1	965	- 011	554	440
2	968	022	485	512
3	958	- 118	775	209
4	937	085	336	630
5	940	311	- 136	999
6	932	247	- 006	970
7	956	- 162	865	117
8	983	- 081	710	300
9	930	- 267	999	- 120
10	988	- 017	578	439
Var'ce	97.0%	3.0%	52.3%	47.7%

The Orthogonal solution throws little light on the nature of the factor pattern other than to show the existence of a large G factor. A graphic display of the Oblique solutions, which reveal a possible second Factor, suggests two categories of rater who use consistently different kinds of rating criteria. A further study, not illustrated above, on a wider range of judges from the initial essay rating points up this dichotomy. A closer study of the rating processes of the differing groups would clarify the nature of subjective rating processes.

Index

Note: All Examination Boards are also mentioned in Fig 4.1 (pp 16-19) and Fig 7.1 (p 95).

Notes

Notes

Notes

Notes

Notes

Notes

Notes